An Inventory of Shimmers

An Inventory of Shimmers

Objects of Intimacy in Contemporary Art

Henriette Huldisch

With contributions by Eugenie Brinkema,
Johanna Burton, and Emily Watlington

DelMonico Books • Prestel   Munich, London, New York

MIT List Visual Arts Center   Cambridge, Massachusetts

CONTENTS

Objects and intimacy comprise so much of daily life. In fact, they often go unquestioned because they are so common. The twelve international artists in *An Inventory of Shimmers: Objects of Intimacy in Contemporary Art* reflect on that which is familiar. Curator Henriette Huldisch has brought together works by Andrea Büttner, Sophie Calle, Alejandro Cesarco, Jason Dodge, Felix Gonzalez-Torres, Antonia Hirsch, Jill Magid, Park McArthur, Lisa Tan, Erika Vogt, Susanne M. Winterling, and Anicka Yi to consider our intimate relations with and through objects.

An Inventory of Shimmers addresses the recent turn toward *affect*—variously defined as forces of encounter, sensations, even emotions. But the work shown is neither sentimental nor melodramatic; instead, it reveals affect to be a part of daily life. Gonzalez-Torres and Calle serve as anchors for a younger generation of artists. Intimacy is a timeless subject, though more attention has been paid to stronger sensations like love. While we are often inclined to seek novel sensations, the ubiquity of intimacy and its objects is precisely what constitutes their pertinence.

This catalogue documents the exhibition at the List Visual Arts Center, on view May 19 through July 16, 2017. Huldisch's astute organiza-tion of the exhibition elucidates concepts of intimacy by considering affects such as vulnera-bility, shame, and desire as integral components, and by considering intimacy through quotidian objects so as to reveal its pervasiveness and examine its forms. Yet while the exhibition's

clarity provides tools for rethinking the familiar, it refuses to diminish intimacy to any sort of formula or theory. For though there is much convergence over how intimacy is experienced, it is also immensely personal. The hotel sheets in Dodge's *Anyone*, which are rotated in the gallery on a weekly basis, have borne witness to many intimate encounters, reminding us that some of our most personal and vulnerable moments are not as individualistic as we think they are, and yet, they remain purely our own.

We are enormously grateful to the lenders and supporters of this exhibition; their generosity has enabled our audience in Boston to peer into Calle's empty safes as they await the secrets of their collecting couple, to glimpse an intimate view inside a convent in Büttner's *Little Things*, and to view slides collected by the elusive architect Luis Barragán in Magid's plea to his archivist.

This elegantly designed catalogue offers significant scholarly contributions to the discourse of affect by way of the artworks on display. Essays authored by Eugenie Brinkema, Johanna Burton, Emily Watlington, and the curator provide insight into intimacy, its related affects and objects, and the projects on view. It was a great pleasure to collaborate with Henriette and all involved in the mounting of this exhibition, which carries forward the List Center's aim of presenting thoughtful, inspiring works of art.

Paul C. Ha
Director

ACKNOWLEDGMENTS

An Inventory of Shimmers: Objects of Intimacy in Contemporary Art was inspired by an interest in considering our affective relationships with and through works of art. In trying to articulate a number of phenomena that elude language or representation, this project from the outset presented an oxymoronic enterprise of sorts. The exhibition is ultimately about ambiguity, nuance, and the value of immaterial things. As it opens in a much harsher political climate than it was conceived in, I hope the artworks in this presentation stake a claim of heightened resonance and weight. It has been my great privilege and pleasure to work with Andrea Büttner, Sophie Calle, Alejandro Cesarco, Jason Dodge, the estate of Felix Gonzalez-Torres, Antonia Hirsch, Jill Magid, Park McArthur, Lisa Tan, Erika Vogt, Susanne M. Winterling, and Anicka Yi in the making of this show.

The exhibition would not have been possible without the generous support of the Andy Warhol Foundation for the Visual Arts, Jane and Neil Pappalardo, Terry and Rick Stone, and Cynthia and John Reed.

Deep thanks go to the lenders who generously shared their works with audiences in Cambridge and beyond: Casey Kaplan Gallery, New York; David Kordansky Gallery, Los Angeles; ESSEX STREET, New York; the Felix Gonzalez-Torres Foundation; Galleri Riis, Oslo; Alex Hank; Nasiba and Thomas Hartland-Mackie; Marguerite Steed Hoffman; Hollybush Gardens, London; Labor, Mexico City; Overduin & Co., Los Angeles; Paula Cooper Gallery, New York; Republic Gallery, Vancouver; Carlomar Rios; Tanya Leighton Gallery, Berlin; Fern and Lenard Tessler; Untilthen, Paris; several of the artists themselves; and a private collection that wishes to remain anonymous.

I thank Eugenie Brinkema and Johanna Burton for authoring their catalogue texts under impossibly short deadlines and for being all-around brilliant. Emily Watlington contributed the invaluable "Index of Intimacy" to the book. Many thanks to Mary DelMonico at DelMonico Books • Prestel for partnering with the List as publishers on this project. Miko McGinty, Rita Jules, and Claire Bidwell outdid themselves once again with the elegant catalogue design, capturing the ambiguity and ephemerality of many works in the exhibition. Anne Ray's editing was fast, furious, and flawless.

I am grateful to the artists' galleries—47 Canal, New York; Casey Kaplan Gallery; David Kordansky Gallery; ESSEX STREET; Galleri Riis; Hollybush Gardens; Labor; Overduin & Co.; Paula Cooper Gallery; Republic Gallery; Tanya Leighton Gallery; and Untilthen—for their responsiveness and assistance throughout the project.

This exhibition, as all List Center presentations, would not be possible without the ardent backing of director Paul C. Ha. Furthermore, I want to thank all of my colleagues for their enthusiasm for the project, and for holding down the fort during my protracted absence while writing the catalogue essay. In particular, I owe thanks again to curatorial research assistant Emily Watlington for her insightful contributions and tireless commitment; this exhibition would not be the same without her. Exhibition manager Tim Lloyd and preparator John Osorio-Buck were at their usual best in installing the works of art; I also thank the eminently capable registrars, Inês Costa Dias and Ariana Webber. And my sincere appreciation to Susie Allen, Karen S. Fegley, Magda Fernandez, Emily A. Garner, Kristin Johnson, Mark Linga, Tricia Murray, Amy Patacchiola, Kelly T. Sherman, Kevin Smith, Yuri Stone, Suara Welitoff, and Betsy Willett for their unfailing diligence and support throughout. Research undertaken by former curatorial fellows Jeffrey De Blois and Monica Steinberg was instrumental in the early stages of developing the exhibition.

Additionally, I thank Andy Graydon for the conversations that sparked the idea for the show and for all of his support along the way.

I save my brightest thanks for the artists themselves, whose passion and commitment never fail to inspire. They graciously took a chance on my inexplicable concept, and I am proud and fortunate to present them in the exhibition it became. Their works shine all on their own.

Henriette Huldisch
Curator

An Inventory of Shimmers:
Objects of Intimacy in Contemporary Art

HENRIETTE HULDISCH

In his final lecture course at the Collège de France, a characteristically elliptical exploration of concepts described as examples of "the neutral," Roland Barthes declared up front that he had developed his ideas alongside a number of readings from "his vacation home," where "the loss in methodological rigor is compensated by the intensity and the pleasure of free reading."[1] From that library, he unapologetically continued, "I made some very arbitrary choices."[2] Barthes's professed unorthodoxy in matters of methodology probably bears more similarity to the working methods of artists than academics.[3] Perhaps more pertinently, I admit that Barthes's irreverence has struck a particular chord during the organization of the exhibition *An Inventory of Shimmers: Objects of Intimacy in Contemporary Art*, which brings together works by artists Andrea Büttner, Sophie Calle, Alejandro Cesarco, Jason Dodge, Felix Gonzalez-Torres, Antonia Hirsch, Jill Magid, Park McArthur, Lisa Tan, Erika Vogt, Susanne M. Winterling, and Anicka Yi. The idea for this show, originally inspired by notions of affect, had percolated over a few years; it was sparked by a more intuitive rather than fully articulated sense of a range of contemporary practices that engage in various ways with modes of address and content that are tethered to affect, emotion, or feeling, yet at the same are wary of lapsing into sentimentality or expressivity.

Delving into the field of affect theory, or the so-called "affective turn," which gained currency beginning in the 1990s, means entering a wildly diverse set of ideas and disciplines. In fact, in their introduction to *The Affect Theory Reader* (2010), Melissa Gregg and Gregory J. Seigworth note that "first encounters with theories of affect might feel like a momentary (sometimes more permanent) methodological and conceptual free fall."[4] Their text is titled after Barthes's evocative phrase *an inventory of shimmers* used in *The Neutral*—a phrase that I have in turn borrowed for the exhibition title—to characterize the shifting, slippery, glittering territory of theorizing affect. As Barthes himself puts it, "the inventory of shimmers is of nuances, of states, of changes . . ."[5] Thus, in the most general sense, the idea of *affect* in relationship to the works of art in this exhibition is interested in exploring how bodies—human or nonhuman—are shaped, modified, or affected by the intensity of their interactions. More specifically, harnessing ideas put forth by affect theory offers, I would argue, a useful if appropriately loose framework in which to think about our entangled, intimate relationships with and through works of art.

In his *Ethics*, published in 1677, philosopher Baruch Spinoza introduced the term as one of his key concepts: "By affect I understand affections of the body by which the body's power of acting is increased or diminished, aided or restrained, and at the same time, the ideas of these affections."[6] His ideas presented a critique of the Cartesian separation of body and mind, and the attendant primacy of reason. In his rejoinder, Spinoza postulated, "No one has yet determined what the body can do."[7] This much-quoted epithet is arguably as elusive as it has been influential to an anti-Cartesian countertradition of thought carried forward by thinkers including Alfred North Whitehead, Henri Bergson, Gilles Deleuze and Félix Guattari, and many others. Over the last twenty or so years the notion of affect has emerged across the humanities and social sciences, where scholars have reconsidered various modes of acquiring knowledge and experience as fundamentally enmeshed with our somatic and emotive selves. Take, for example, the pioneering work of Eve Kosofsky Sedgwick and Adam Frank in their reading of psychologist Silvan Tomkins and his theory of nine biologically anchored affects as motivating factors for human behavior (a theory specifically distinguished from Sigmund Freud's concept of drives); Brian Massumi's adaptation of Deleuzian intensities into disrupting, dynamic states of "incipience" containing the potential of political action; or concepts of "affective labor"—that is, forms of work related to producing or transforming nontangible, emotional states, as well as care work—as developed by Michael Hardt and Antonio Negri.[8] In a recent conversation, sociologist and cultural theorist Christoph Behnke divided the field broadly into two paradigms (Gregg and Seigworth, by contrast, parse out six strands):

> On one hand we have the theories that relate affects to inner psychic realities, to structures of instinct or affects anchored in our physical bodies, which are installed like hardware . . . including neuroscientific writings in which affects are always accompanied by a physical substrate. In contrast, all the approaches to the study of emotion that we find in sociology . . . locate the production of emotions in interactive relationships, in chains of interaction, that take on a life of their own and can also carry individuals away in the sense of a mutual entrainment.[9]

One of the key points not brought out fully by this description is the notion that modes of affect are not—or not fully—conscious and, hence, prelinguistic.[10]

On the surface, none of this may seem like a particularly obvious milieu for the so-called visual arts, yet different thinkers working on affect have been tremendously resonant with contemporary artists, curators, and critics alike.

One explanation for affect theory's appeal across disciplines is a sense of exhaustion vis-à-vis a long-running academic reign of textuality and linguistics (roughly contemporaneous with the rise of Minimalism and Conceptualism, incidentally). Add to this a consistent privileging of cognitive and visual engagement with works of art at the expense of the other senses. As artist Yi stated in a recent conversation, "Everything is about looking—we have such ocular fatigue . . . I believe we've lost our empathetic core because we've neglected these other senses, like smell and touch and taste."[11] The notion that conceptual art was never as emotionally cool as some would have it is a contention put forth in the 2007 exhibition *Romantic Conceptualism*.[12] This show traced romantic motifs in works by artists such as Bas Jan Ader, Gonzalez-Torres, Yoko Ono, Adrian Piper, Lawrence Weiner, and others from the 1960s onward, and proposed that affective or emotional charge and conceptual premise were never incompatible to begin with.[13]

Cultural studies scholar Jennifer Doyle has recently leveled a related charge at the contemporary art world in describing a stultifying tendency toward habitual critical detachment. In *Hold It Against Me: Difficulty and Emotion in Contemporary Art*, she proposes: "Art criticism has aligned one form of difficulty (in which a work's meaning is not readily available to the viewer) with a regulation of affect (in which opacity, the difficulty of meaning, is packaged as cool, distanced, and anti-emotional)," so that as a result, "for the fully initiated such works don't feel very hard at all."[14] Admittedly, the artists and works she discusses in her text are for the most part very different from the ones included in *An Inventory of Shimmers*—for example, Ron Athey and his visceral performances involving extreme self-modification. But her point is a trenchant one. Put somewhat differently, looking at and thinking about works of art solely in terms of perceptual and spatial relationships obviously cuts out a huge chunk of what makes up human experience.

Curators' and artists' interest in affect and affect theory has partly dovetailed with theories of objects and their "inner lives" as formulated under the rubrics of speculative realism and object-oriented ontology.[15] Delving into these philosophies is clearly beyond the scope of this essay or exhibition (not to mention it would entail a methodological and theoretical free fall unto its own), however, the idea that objects exist—have causality and action independent of human cognition or perception— for somewhat obvious reasons strikes a chord for artists and art professionals, who spend their lives making, looking at, and thinking about objects (though, of course, many contemporary artworks are not objects in the strict sense, or at all). The intellectual interest in the potential secret lives of objects resonates with affect by way of a (renewed) legitimacy in thinking about our magical relationship with things. Cultural studies scholar Cornelia Kastelan describes "the presumption that in art, beyond allocation of meaning—in other words the classical way of interpreting pictures—activations are created which are not cognitively controlled but are also affective in the sense that they involve an overpowering interplay of picture and observer, and which are caused by circulating emotions . . . Obviously, here a return to the idea of the 'magic' of pictures is taking place."[16]

The current interest in affect is almost certainly propounded by our living environment, ever more defined by the network and disembodied forms of communication and interaction, which, perhaps only logically, not only prompt a reconsideration of our relationship to physical objects but amplify the interest in empathy, emotion, and intimacy in the other. This, artist Hito Steyerl writes, is "an age in which data, feelings, and touch travel lightly."[17] Importantly, newer modes of communication not dependent on physical presence do not preclude intimacy. It would be misguided to assume that e-mail, texting, and so forth present an unprecedented redefinition of human intimacy, as if people haven't had intensely intimate relationships by writing letters or speaking on the phone in the past. Rather, what's at stake is that digital technologies are increasingly blurring the boundaries between human and machine behavior, between where the body ends and the machine begins. Spike Jonze's 2013 film *Her*, about a man who falls in love with his computer's operating system, may be science fiction, but just barely so.

The exhibition *An Inventory of Shimmers* is situated at the juncture of these ideas around affect. However, to echo Barthes's indifference toward theoretical purity, quoted above, my approach has been to act rather like a spy in the house Baruch built. The show does not adhere to or illustrate any particular affect theory, neither does it aim to make strict delineations between affect, emotion, and feeling. That said, the works here are very far from melodrama or emotional excess, both of which are anything but unconscious. This is also not an exhibition that talks about an enveloping kind of full sensory address characteristic of much immersive installation made since the 1990s.[18] Rather, the show focuses on intimacy instead, which is necessarily affective. Intimacy requires some kind of reciprocity between discrete entities, proximity (actual or felt), and trust. The works brought together in the exhibition variously and in ways that overlap investigate our intimate relationships with objects, act as vehicles for affective engagement or transactions of desire between people, or are directly engaged with actions of care, trust, and love. Many objects in the exhibition carry the traces of things we can't see but have to trust, intuit, or perceive in ways that are not related to vision or hearing—thus, the themes of the cerebral, the sensory, and the spectral are intertwined.

Gonzalez-Torres functions as a point of departure and center of gravity in the exhibition. Throughout his work, the artist combined formal economy and conceptual rigor with deeply affecting content. Piles of candy left in the gallery for the visitors' taking, curtains made from translucent fabric or glittering beads, and sparse wall works typically conceal depths of desire, anger, and loss.[19] Many of Gonzalez-Torres's works are portraits of or homages to his partner, Ross Laycock, who died from complications of AIDS in 1991. *"Untitled" (Loverboy)* (1989), the only historical work in *An Inventory of Shimmers*, is surely one of them. One in a series of curtain pieces that have to be fabricated each time they are shown, the work consists of light-blue fabric installed in front of a gallery window. The window can be open or closed. Besides the title, only the color blue here attests to the visually restrained work's emotional, and possibly spiritual, underpinnings. In a 1994 review of a show at the Renaissance Society, Alan G. Artner notes that the use of light blue throughout makes allusion to a baby boy's blanket, an item the artist's family could not afford.[20] Blue, in English, is associated with melancholy, and in German romanticism a blue flower symbolizes longing and infinity. More to the point, light blue is associated with the sky (and by extension heaven). As this work was made during a time when the artist's partner was already very ill, it is difficult to not read the curtains and windows as connected with death, with passing from materiality to immateriality, with the "fluttering of souls."[21] In Victorian England clocks would be stopped and curtains drawn upon a person's death.

Calle's work, rooted firmly in our personal connections in the here and now, forms another anchor to the exhibition. From the beginning of her career Calle has made herself deliberately vulnerable in and through her work, exposing her own intimate affairs and pursuits, as well as those of others: she has photographed strangers' belongings while working as a chambermaid in Venice (*The Hotel*, 1983) and asked 107 professional women to analyze, annotate, or perform a "breakup e-mail" sent to her by a former lover (*Take Care of Yourself*, 2007). *Secrets* (2014), which Eugenie Brinkema discusses in ingenious detail in her contribution to this publication, is less a set of material objects than it is a contract and an assertion of trust. Two secrets are locked inside two safes; each belongs to one of the work's owners (a couple). The contents consist of something the other person doesn't know about and, presumably, is not supposed to know—yet Calle knows. The artist places the secrets, each written on a piece of paper, inside the safes herself. As such, Calle is a double agent: confidante and conspirator to both owners. The work not only concretizes the notion that all our personal relationships are shaped by secrets (by who does and doesn't know something), but also that secrets usually come with the desire to tell (after all, the best way to keep a secret is to keep it to yourself).

Magid has followed in Calle's footsteps in some of her works, instigating and interloping into intimate relationships. She is interested in control and complicity, the implicit contractual underpinnings of interpersonal interactions, and conversely, the intimate substrate of institutional relationships. "Permission is a pact, a covenant. It binds the institution and me together, and thus has the potential for intimacy," she says.[22] *Dearest Federica* (2013) is part of her ongoing project *The Barragán Archives*, in which she has forged a sort of ménage à trois between the modernist architect Luis Barragán, architecture scholar Federica Zanco, and herself. After being denied access to Barragán's professional archive, which was acquired by the CEO of the Swiss Vitra company (Zanco's then-fiance, now-husband) and is owned by the Barragan Foundation[23] subsequently set up, Magid began to delve into Barragán's work, using his designs while meticulously respecting the foundation's copyright restrictions. She also initiated a series of epistolary appeals to Zanco.[24] The slides comprising *Dearest Federica* are striking photographs of young women Magid found in Barragán's personal archive (which has remained in Mexico and is open to the public). In the accompanying voiceover, Magid reads a letter combining her own writing with excerpts from a letter Barragán wrote to a lover: "As you well know, my dear Federica, my greatest desire, a fantastical and immensely ambitious desire, is to fully understand you even in your most secret thoughts." In response to Zanco's repeated rebuffs (she claims to safeguard the papers while she is completing the architect's catalogue raisonné), Magid, as jilted conceptual artist, has ardently pursued the architect and his self-appointed guardian. What was originally an entirely one-sided affair has since become a kind of exchange, as Zanco has publicly commented on Magid's work; what's more, Magid continues to write herself into both of their stories.

McArthur's sculptural assemblages *Contact C*, *Contact S*, and *Contact T* (all 2016) consist of stainless-steel trays, mounted on short plinths, filled with a range of prophylactic and hygienic items: catheters, latex gloves, swabs, masks, cannulas, and more. Her accumulations of readymade objects call to mind Gonzalez-Torres's take-away candy piles, such as *"Untitled" (Portrait of Ross in L.A.)* (1991), and the mundane medical items similarly conjure an absent body.[25] However, McArthur's works directly reference illness or disability, while the specter of AIDS is implicit in Gonzalez-Torres's. And the *Contact* pieces, in fact, always refer to two or more bodies. The items on display are variously used to penetrate and protect the body's boundaries—actions that necessarily entail a specific kind of physical proximity, although they are not often or usually intimate ones. At the same time, this proximity contains the possibility of intimacy, and McArthur's work resides in that liminal space. Writer and disability justice activist Mia Mingus has put forward the idea of "access intimacy," which is "that elusive, hard to describe feeling when someone else 'gets' your access needs."[26] The *Contact* works also "challenge our ideas about where the body ends and where its surroundings and supports begin," as Amelia Groom remarks, making reference to ideas drawing on lived experiences advanced in the field of disability studies.[27] That recasting of boundaries further insists on the necessary interconnectedness of sensory, mental, and affective states. McArthur's work as a whole is concerned with a related set of larger ideas considering normative definitions of sovereignty and dependence, and accessibility and its personal, social, and political implications.

Different notions of reciprocity and care run through Büttner's video *Little Works* (2007). The piece, which follows a group of Carmelite nuns in a London convent, is concerned with community, spiritual and otherwise, and a certain kind of mindfulness expressed through objects. The video documents the women's activities as they make scented sachets, baskets, candles, and so forth in preparation of their annual celebration. The nuns call these objects their "little works," yet however modest, the items also function as something like tokens of a collective commitment to a set of shared beliefs and faith. As one of the sisters says, what is at the heart of their fair is "that lovely atmosphere of community and everyone taking an interest in what everyone else has done." Büttner has gravitated toward ostensibly "minor" or "unfashionable" topics and techniques throughout much of her work; as Brian Dillon describes, she engages with "a complex set of historical ideas about wealth and poverty, shame and dignity, the relationship of art to one's form of life."[28] In Tomkins's psychological framework, shame is a fundamental affect, and Büttner makes implicit reference to the idea in displaying her works in front of a "shit wall." This is a wall painted brown up to approximately where the artist's hand can reach so that it is demarcated by an uneven line above eye level. The color obviously references bodily waste with all its shameful social connotations; in that, the work becomes an emphatic expression of Büttner's embrace of exposure and embarrassment as a source of artistic and ethical possibility. If she asserts what Martin Herbert calls "the virtues of vulnerability," these always encompass the vulnerability involved in exhibiting works of art as such.[29]

Hirsch explores our direct visceral relationships with material objects against the backdrop of immaterial communication and digital culture. "Important to the notion that use-objects may be 'magically' charged is the affective hapticity of objects," she states.[30] The installation *Object T* (2015) comprises a video of two women (one of them shown on a screen within the screen) in medium close-up as they examine a smooth, black cube. Both speak in a low voice, deliberately turning and stroking the small object bathed in a soft yellow light that evokes the aesthetic of Dutch still-life painting. But the sculpture involves a more fully physical experience as the spectator is seated on a heated granite bench. The bench's smooth surface echoes that of the cube, and its dimensions correspond to those of the screen. The work also riffs on amateur ASMR videos posted on YouTube. ASMR, or autonomous sensory meridian response, refers to a set of "tingly" and relaxing sensations triggered in some people by soft or whispering voices, the handling and tapping of objects, actions of care and grooming, and more.[31] Hirsch recognizes the peculiar phenomenon (or better, its mediatization online) as a node where affect, intimacy, immateriality, and materiality coalesce. Some of the scenarios watched on the screen, while wearing headphones, are intensely intimate.[32] However, Hirsch is more interested in the curious slippage between community service and commerce enacted through ASMR videos: advertised as free tools to combat stress and insomnia (that are reportedly effective), they are also unofficial product endorsements for items demonstrated in makeup tutorials or "unboxing" videos.[33] As such, ASMR videos may represent the epitome of affective labor.

Vogt's room installation *Secret Traveler Navigator* (2010) includes a projection inside a black space (painted in thick enamel) that unfolds like a magic trick, a ritual, or an incantation. Filmed like a shadow play, it presents a succession of silhouetted figures handling mysterious objects against backgrounds of changing colors. The voiceover introduces a narrator, "a man of shimmering devices [who] in the middle of his story, has lost his way." Vogt's piece does indeed tell an elliptical kind of narrative, where different characters—capitalist, artist, charlatan—are represented through their objects. However, its meaning and resolution are elusive, just as the stylized devices themselves, repeatedly held up or passed back and forth between two sets of hands, accompanied by a hypnotic voiceover, remain ambiguous. The "actual" objects used in the film are scattered on the floor throughout the darkened space; as such, the installation functions like a kind of Platonic cave, with fugitive apparition on the screen and physical manifestation in space. In fact, Vogt's work negotiates a number of such juxtapositions, oscillating between distance and closeness, illusion and reality, magic and the mundane.

Dodge's work *Anyone* consists of stacks of folded, clean bed sheets that are interspersed throughout the gallery and exchanged weekly by a commercial linen service. Divorced from their regular duties and settings, the utilitarian items become curious objects: They are at once uncomfortably intimate, having been slept on by many different people in a hotel, and completely anonymous, regularly laundered and stripped of their users' physical traces. *Anyone* also presents something of an inverse to related works like *The Children Are Sleeping* and *The Ornithologists Are Sleeping*, which constitute pillows displayed on the floor that have been slept on by a single person of the titular group. In those works, the sleepers are presumably still present in whatever bodily residue has been left on the pillow, yet they are not perceptible, or only perceptible on a subliminal level.[34] Dodge's works often pivot on the presence of something that can't be seen, although, as he has said, "it could potentially be present in exhibitions on a molecular level."[35] In short, this presence is something that has to be trusted. How do we know that anyone has slept on anything, hotel linens or pillows? Significantly, we don't. We have to take the artist's word for it.

Cesarco's *Fragile Images That Keep Producing Death While Attempting to Preserve Life: Flowers found in crime scenes_001–004* (2011) consists of four black-and-white photographs of flowers. Closely cropped, the views disclose little of their surroundings, except for a white picket fence in one the images, and the siding of a house in the background of another. Although these elements suggest the pictures were taken outside, the flowers (some of them wilting) call to mind *vanitas* paintings and their symbols of mortality. But as the title indicates, these pictures are actually steeped in death. Cesarco has appropriated newspaper images from scenes of violent crimes and eliminated everything except the flowers. As in Gonzalez-Torres's work, Cesarco's minimal aesthetic—his strategies of withholding, absence, invisibility—cloaks affective and romantic underpinnings. The flower images are as much about what they don't show (a crime and possibly death). In the context of the *Inventory of Shimmers* exhibition, the photographs introduce the relative proximity of animate and inanimate things. Plants are living beings, although not sentient ones. What does it mean, if it means anything, for a flower to witness a death? Whether a plant could be in some dim and diffuse neurobiological way affected by an act of violence is of course speculative. However, the viewers' recognition that these flowers have been close to a human death makes all the difference, cognitively and perhaps affectively. That is, if we trust Cesarco's claim about the compositions' origins in the first place.

In her recent works, Yi has been concerned with notions of the hybrid: between human, animal, and plant; the animate and inanimate; and the organic and inorganic. A series of wall works she refers to as "chicken skins" contain artificial flowers mounted in a frame of stretched silicone in sickly shades of yellow, pink, brown, and violet. Despite the artificiality of the material, however, these surfaces appear fleshy and are pocked with goosebumps (they were actually cast from ostrich skin).[36] Yi has stated her desire to "reorder the senses," which has in earlier works taken the form of using different manufactured fragrances, or setting off processes of bacterial growth or material decay, with all of their attendant scents.[37] These newer works do not address our olfactory sense, but they do register viscerally. The chicken skins gesture toward how different species experience bodily affections, in ways very similar and different.[38] Goosebumps are caused by cold, as well as intense emotions like fear, disgust, and arousal; they are, in short, affective. They are also not unique to humans, although in animals reflexively raised fur or feathers, presumably, retain the function of scaring off predators. Yi's amalgamation of human, animal, and plant characteristics in these works throws their ontological and hierarchical delineations into question. How animate does something have to be to warrant empathy? And when is something so close to inanimateness that it causes disgust instead?

A similar set of questions has motivated Winterling's recent work. For a number of years she has studied the microscopic marine organisms called dinoflagellates. These protists are bioluminescent: when mechanically activated— by the movement of swimmers or boats, for example—populations of dinoflagellates cause a blue glow in the water. Philosopher Karen Barad—whose work positing the fundamental entanglement and interdependency of all things, human and nonhuman, is a key influence for Winterling—cites "dinos" as one instance of "queer" nature: for one, they "are neither plant nor animal, but can act as both."[39] Winterling calls the bioluminescent dinoflagellates and the ecosystems in which they are embedded an "affective, haptic system."[40] The teeny organisms react to touch in a way the artist compares to a living touchscreen. In this, she, much like Yi, deliberately blurs the lines between the human hand, shiny technology, and plankton. For *Vertex (Metabolic)* (2015), Winterling created a 3-D print of a single dinoflagellate, enlarged to the point where it resembles a jellyfish. The sculpture is suspended inside a white box and illuminated by black light. The viewer is put at actual and metaphorical eye level with the organism, albeit one that doesn't have eyes or a central nervous system. Winterling's sculpture thus presents a knowingly outlandish model considering the possibility of interspecies communication and the limits of empathy.

If *An Inventory of Shimmers* opens, conceptually, with Gonzalez-Torres's "*Untitled*" curtains, Tan's video installation *Waves* (2014–15) forms its summation. Shown on a hanging screen inside a room with blue walls and carpet, Tan's video intertwines reflections on Virginia Woolf's novel *The Waves* (1931), jellyfish, submarine cables, data centers, Gustave Courbet's painting *The Wave* (1869), Google Art & Culture, and more. At heart, the work wrestles with a paradox that haunts theories of affect and this exhibition alike: How do you describe or picture "whatever is lurking behind thought," as Tan narrates, borrowing from Clarice Lispector, something that is unconscious and prelinguistic? Her subjects all represent attempts to articulate the ungraspable, as, for example, Woolf's text fusing multiple narrators into a "continuous stream, not solely of human thought." She considers communication by Skype, paradoxically abstract and matter-of-fact at the same time, while describing the material reality of data servers that are cooled with water drawn from the Baltic Sea. Throughout, Tan's project is concerned with liminalities: between water and land, language and nonlanguage, consciousness and subconsciousness. Rather than describing them, however, the piece aims to take liminal form itself, taking its cue from Woolf's text or Courbet's painting trying to fix the break of a wave. "I feel as though jellyfish have it down best," says Tan in voiceover. "Their formlessness leads them to encounters with the source of any given thing." Parsing the links between such formless entities as water, data, pixels, and emotions, Tan doesn't accord any of them greater or lesser material and ontological gravity. All resemble shimmering affects that lap at the edge of consciousness like waves.

Notes

1 Barthes, *The Neutral: Lecture Course at the Collège de France (1977–78)*, trans. Rosalind E. Krauss and Denis Hollier (New York: Columbia University Press, 2005), 9.

2 Ibid.

3 In fact, I would argue that much of contemporary art's current popularity (theoretical absurdities and conceits notwithstanding) owes at least in part to the fact that it presents a wide open intellectual playing field where artists freely draw on any number of disciplines, in ways that can be exceedingly rigorous and not.

4 Gregg and Seigworth, "An Inventory of Shimmers," in *The Affect Theory Reader*, ed. Gregg and Seigworth (Durham, NC: Duke University Press, 2010), 1.

5 Barthes, *The Neutral*, 77.

6 Spinoza, *Ethics*, trans. Stuart Hampshire and E. M. Curley (London: Penguin Books, 1996), 157.

7 Ibid., 161.

8 See Sedgwick and Frank, "Shame in the Cybernetic Fold: Reading Silvan Tomkins," *Critical Inquiry* 21, no. 2 (winter 1995): 496–522; Cornelia Kastelan in "Affect, Attachment, and Passion—An Exchange between Christoph Behnke, Cornelia Kastelan, and Ulf Wuggenig," in *Art in the Periphery of the Center*, ed. Behnke, Kastelan, and Wuggenig (Berlin: Sternberg Press, 2015), 42; Massumi, *Parables for the Virtual: Movement, Affect, Sensation* (Durham, NC: Duke University Press, 2002); and Hardt and Negri, *Multitude: War and Democracy in the Age of Empire* (New York: Penguin, 2004).

9 Behnke, Kastelan, and Wuggenig, eds., *Art in the Periphery of the Center*, 48.

10 However, the cited interest in conceptualizing direct affective relationships with (aesthetic) objects as connected with our neuro-physiological makeup in neuroscience clearly exceeds the scope of this text.

11 Karen Rosenberg, "Scent of 100 Women: Artist Anicka Yi on Her New Viral Feminism Campaign at the Kitchen," *Artspace*, March 12, 2015, accessed January 19, 2016, http://www.artspace.com/magazine/interviews_features/meet_the_artist/scent-of-100-women-anicka-yis-viral-feminism-52678.

12 Mounted at Kunsthalle Nürnberg (May 10–July 15, 2007) and BAWAG P.S.K. Contemporary, Vienna (September 14–December 1, 2007), curated by art critic Jörg Heiser.

13 Art historian Eve Meltzer recently made a related argument examining 1960s art with recourse to affect theory in *Systems We Have Loved: Conceptual Art, Affect, and the Antihumanist Turn* (Chicago: Chicago University Press, 2013).

14 Doyle, *Hold It Against Me: Difficulty and Emotion in Contemporary Art* (Durham, NC: Duke University Press, 2013), xvii, 8.

15 See Christoph Cox, Jenny Jaskey, and Suhail Malik, eds., *Realism Materialism Art* (Annandale-on-Hudson, NY: Center for Curatorial Studies, Bard College; Berlin: Sternberg Press, 2015).

16 Behnke, Kastelan, and Wuggenig, eds., *Art in the Periphery of the Center*, 49.

17 Steyerl, "Epistolary Affect and Romance Scams: Letter from an Unknown Woman," in *2013 Carnegie International*, ed. Daniel Baumann, Dan Byers, and Tina Kukielski (Pittsburgh: Carnegie Museum of Art, Carnegie Institute, 2013), 249.

18 See Claire Bishop, *Installation Art: A Critical History* (New York: Routledge, 2005), 6. Bishop states that "installation art presupposes an *embodied* viewer whose senses of touch, smell, and sound are as heightened as their sense of vision. The insistence on the literal presence of the viewer is arguably the key characteristic of installation art."

19 "Ross Bleckner and Felix Gonzalez-Torres," *BOMB* no. 51 (spring 1995), 47. Gonzalez-Torres was explicit about a strategy of veiling; in an interview conducted a year before his untimely death, he said to artist Bleckner: "Some homophobic senator is going to have a very hard time trying to explain to his constituency that my work is homoerotic or pornographic."

20 Artner, "Moving Minimalism," *Chicago Tribune*, October 23, 1994, accessed January 26, 2017, http://articles.chicagotribune.com/1994-10-23/entertainment/9410230138_1_gonzalez-torres-renaissance-society-viewers.

21 Ibid.

22 Jeff Edwards, "Permission Is a Material: An Interview with Jill Magid," *Artpulse Magazine*, 2014, accessed January 26, 2017, http://artpulsemagazine.com/permission-is-a-material-an-interview-with-jill-magid.

23 The foundation's name does not include an accent.

24 The project recently found its preliminary culmination in the exhibition *The Proposal* (2016), where Magid presented a diamond ring created from Barragán's ashes to Zanco in exchange for the promise to return the professional papers to Mexico. As of this writing, Zanco has not replied to the proposal. See also Alice Gregory, "The Architect Who Became a Diamond," *New Yorker*, August 1, 2016, accessed January 26, 2017, http://www.newyorker.com/magazine/2016/08/01/how-luis-barragan-became-a-diamond.

25 See Jason Farago, "Sucked Up, Squeezed Out: The Super-Absorbent Art of Park McArthur," *Guardian*, January 26, 2016, accessed January 26, 2017, https://www.theguardian.com/artanddesign/2016/jan/26/park-mcarthur-poly-chisenhale-gallery-london-sculpture-art.

26 Mingus, "Access Intimacy: The Missing Link," *Leaving Evidence*, May 5, 2011, accessed January 24, 2017, https://leavingevidence.wordpress.com/2011/05/05/access-intimacy-the-missing-link/.

27 Groom, "Park McArthur at Chisenhale Gallery," *artforum.com*, accessed January 24, 2017, https://www.artforum.com/picks/id=58879.

28 Dillon, "Embarrassment of Riches," *frieze* 180 (June/July/August 2016), 158.

29 Herbert, "Camcorders, Convents, Collectivism, and Confession," *frieze* 133 (September 2010), 119.

30 Antonia Hirsch, unpublished project description, 2016.

31 This under-researched phenomenon has spawned an Internet culture with millions of viewers. See, for example, Stephanie Fairyington, "Rustle, Tingle, Relax: The Compelling World of A.S.M.R," *New York Times*, July 28, 2016, accessed January 25, 2017, http://well.blogs.nytimes.com/2014/07/28/rustle-tingle-relax-the-compelling-world-of-a-s-m-r/.

32 For example, performers pretend to stroke the viewer's face, brush hair, or whisper in ears.

33 Many producers of ASMR content collect donations, and YouTube's ASMR stars earn money from ads and banners.

34 Both works call to mind Gonzalez-Torres's billboard *"Untitled"* (1991), a black-and-white photograph of an empty bed with crumpled sheets and pillows made after Laycock's death.

35 Lauren O'Neill-Butler, "Jason Dodge," *Artforum* (March 2014), 288.

36 Not coincidentally, silicone isn't strictly speaking a plastic but is made from atoms of silicon, in other words, the main element used in glass.

37 Rosenberg, "Scent of 100 Women."

38 I am indebted to Emily Watlington in helping to formulate these ideas.

39 Barad, "Nature's Queer Performativity," *Qui Parle: Critical Humanities and Social Sciences* 19, no. 2 (spring/summer 2011), 133.

40 Susanne M. Winterling, unpublished project description, 2015.

Story of My Life …

JOHANNA BURTON

According to revolutionary psychologist Silvan Tomkins, core "scenes" within an individual's life, woven together and mapped sequentially, come to comprise that life's *plot*.[1] As the dynamic and shape of a subject's plot emerges, that same subject is busy (if largely unconsciously) constructing "scripts," so many "rules for predicting, interpreting, responding to, and controlling a magnified set of scenes." In other words, the patterns we see in our and others' lives might be understood as resulting equally from overtly determining social contexts and from the tactics we turn to in order to manage them. By and large, however, our scripts—"more self-validating than self-fulfilling"—work as survival strategies, coping mechanisms, negotiations between self and society: between what is felt and what is recognized; between the passionate and the rational; between the fantasy of intimacy and the reality of alienation.[2] They are, too, strange testaments to the incompatibility of the story of any person's life and actual inhabitation of it.

The most important category of scenes and their associated scripts are, terrifyingly, given the nomenclature "nuclear" by Tomkins.[3] Nuclear scenes— repeating and nearly always doomed—come to most forcefully shape human beings, in part because the strength of affect that gathers around them only grows over time, and never in a direction of resolution. In a passage worthy of citation in full, Tomkins describes nuclear scenes this way:

> They are the good scenes we can never totally or permanently achieve or possess. If they occasionally seem to be totally achieved or possessed, such possession can never be permanent. If they reward us with deep positive affect, we are forever greedy for more. If the scenes are good, they may never be good enough, and we are eager for them to be improved and perfected. If they punish us with deep negative affect, we can never entirely avoid, escape, nor renounce the attempt to master or revenge ourselves upon them despite much punishment. If they both seduce and punish us, we can neither possess nor renounce them. If they are conflicted scenes, we can neither renounce wishes of the

conflicting nor integrate them. If they are ambiguous scenes,
we can neither simplify nor clarify the many overlapping scenes
which characteristically produce pluralistic confusion.[4]

An example of a nuclear scene and the script produced to account for and anticipate it is given by Tomkins; in great detail, he shows the way that a man who has experienced ongoing humiliation in his lifetime is confronted one day by unexpected, sincere praise. In no less than eight distinct ways, Tomkins outlines how the man manages to turn admiration into admonition, since it is the only story he knows (some examples: the praise is insincere, it is incorrect, he will never live up to its expectations, etc.). Ironically perhaps, the only way to maintain a sense of self is by reinscribing that self's vulnerabilities and precariousness, and by affirming the very ways it threatens to come undone at the hands of others. For in every instance, scripts—and nuclear scripts above all—are iterations of the oldest story in the world: the desire for and impossibility of intimacy.

That said, intimacy might well be overrated—or at very least misunderstood. Etymologically, it derives from the Latin *intimus*, with earliest meanings tending toward interiority (*intimus* = "inmost"), and only later becoming aligned with deep levels of familiarity *between* people, whether emotional or physical. While a good amount of theoretical and other work has plumbed the complexities of intimacy and the desire for it, there is, however, still a vague general consensus (a long-standing meme?) that it is something to aim for: if not easy, nonetheless essential; if not attainable, nonetheless a pinnacle to aspire toward.[5] Intimacy is so often, as we know, confused with love (and the distinction certainly can be confusing) or commitment, or depth, but it can also be anything but these things. Indeed, if intimacy is often held up as a good object, it is despite so much evidence to the contrary.

A couple of years ago the artist Anicka Yi sent one of her studio assistants to the museum where I work, where he rather unceremoniously fulfilled his task, which was to swab the inside of my cheek with a Q-tip. There was nothing uncouth about the exchange; but for its anonymity (I no longer remember his name) and clinical nature (the moist cotton swab was immediately dispatched into a sealed plastic bag), it was nonetheless intimate. I remember feeling strangely exposed in the public arena of the museum's lobby, and oddly at the mercy of this person who probably felt the same way about me. The bacteria on that swab—as well as on ninety-nine others, each provided by a different woman—was utilized by Yi to produce a fragrance that spoke to the question, what does feminism smell like? The answer: it stank, in a deep, intense, decomposing kind of way. In her refusal to renounce the less flattering caricatures of female solidarity (those perpetuated by patriarchy, for instance), Yi literally created an atmosphere that gave it shrewd new form. By the time audience members realized they had entered an invisible but palpable realm, it was too late: the scent of a woman (!) not only around but inside every body that couldn't help but inhale it.

In her essay "Happy Objects," Sara Ahmed explores the ideological and affective foundations for "good things"—people, places, things, ideas, and constructions that are assigned value. Her wager, radically simplified by me here, is that the maintenance of so-called normative configurations of happiness is reliant on the unhappiness produced by those who disrupt them. Ahmed points to figures including "the feminist kill-joy" and "the angry black woman," among others.[6] "Some bodies," she writes, "are presumed to be the origin of bad feeling insofar as they disturb the promise of happiness, which I would re-describe as the social pressure to maintain the signs of 'getting along.' Some bodies become blockage points, points where smooth communication stops."[7]

I think of other bodies and practices that might be described as enacting such blockage: Nayland Blake's sculpture *Dual Restraint*, a straitjacket fitted for two, insists on the fine (indistinguishable?) line between embrace and entrapment; Park McArthur and Constantina Zavitsanos's "other forms of conviviality" return to rather than repress forms of debt that accrue through and by way of care; and Community Action Center, a collective project spearheaded by A. K. Burns and A. L. Steiner, insists on both erotics and sexuality as inherently political.[8]

I name these three examples, in addition to Yi, as no more than indicators of the multiplicity of artists working against the grain, disavowing the "good things" often taken for granted. But in these disavowals, there are also new models proposed. Indeed, all the artists I've gestured to above, in various ways, overturn hegemonic models of kinship, replacing the nuclear family, as it were, with other kinds of intimate actions, entanglements, and agents. As Ahmed reminds, oppositional strategies yield pleasures, too. The exposure of "unhappy effects" (in this case, deeply binding affiliations outside the white, abled, hetero-normative, middle-classed, patriarchal) can produce, if not happiness (though sometimes it can), transformation, an "alternative set of imaginings of what might count as a good or better life."[9]

In our current moment, of course, it would be hard not to note how the word *nuclear* resonates even more sinisterly than usual, weirdly as a semantic link between possible future (or imminent) world wars and the new administration's heralding a return to "family values." Yet, it is with emphatic—impossibly yet willfully euphoric—insistence that even the most nuclear of nuclear scenes *might* be detoured and that the most nuclear of nuclear scripts *could* be rewritten that some of the most important contemporary artists proceed, suggesting new valences for intimacy in understanding and implementation alike.

Notes

1 Tomkins, *Shame and Its Sisters: A Silvan Tomkins Reader*, ed. Eve Kosofsky Sedgwick and Adam Frank (Durham, NC: Duke University Press, 1995), 180.

2 Ibid., 181.

3 It is worth noting that Tomkins's work on script theory and nuclear scripts was published in 1991, in the third of four volumes he produced specifically dedicated to affect. The first two volumes were published in 1962 and 1963 respectively. Volume three appears after a twenty-eight year pause. The choice of the word *nuclear* at that moment is, I think, notable, especially given Tomkins's overt attention to the political landscape and his having written on affect against the evolving backdrop of the Cold War.

4 Tomkins, *Shame and Its Sisters*, 183–84.

5 For example, see Leo Bersani and Adam Phillips, *intimacies* (Chicago: University of Chicago Press, 2008), and *Intimacy*, ed. Lauren Berlant (Chicago: University of Chicago Press, 2000). Both volumes trouble easy ideas of intimacy and challenge the conventions of and expectations mapped onto it.

6 Ahmed, "Happy Objects," in *The Affect Theory Reader*, ed. Melissa Gregg and Gregory J. Seigworth (Durham, NC: Duke University Press, 2010), 38–39.

7 Ibid., 39.

8 See McArthur and Zavitsanos, "Other forms of conviviality: The best and least of which is our daily care and the host of which is our collaborative work," in *Women & Performance* 23, no. 1, accessed March 10, 2017, https://www .womenandperformance.org /ampersand/ampersand -articles/other-forms-of -conviviality.html.

9 Ahmed, "Happy Objects," 50. Lauren Berlant, too, meditates on the ways people often desire the very things that work against their best interests, happiness, and well-being. Her focus is, particularly, the construction of the "good life" put forward by a liberal democracy that withholds it for most. See Berlant, *Cruel Optimism* (Durham, NC: Duke University Press, 2011).

26, more or less:
Sophie Calle's *Secrets*

EUGENIE BRINKEMA

Assumptions

It assumes that there are lovers.

It assumes that some lovers have secrets.

It assumes that those secrets can be put into words.

It assumes that each lover will have only one secret worth keeping, or (a) an overriding secret among minor, trivial, or banal ones that renders choosing the critical one neither impossible nor of such difficulty that one quickly abandons the effort; or (b) a few secrets of some brevity, which, quickly ordered, amount to an assemblage of secrets, forming perhaps a meta-secret, so once more we are in the territory of the one; or (c) several secrets of equivalent merit and not of any particular brevity but of a form such that with a bit of editing or a slackening paraphrase it might be possible, and without losing the long line, to give each quickly, which is to say succinctly, so as to ensure that they might fit into a safe of 20-by-25-by-20 centimeters, which, all told, is not a large amount of space.

It assumes that these lovers would find it frustrating, agonizing—grating, at least—to live behind Vaseline-glazed glass knowing they cannot see all clearly, in proximity to the material reminder of the partner's intimate life, to see the physical manifestation of a distance from each other, measured in the sliver of wall separating the safes and given at the remove of this slip of language. Rephrase as: it assumes that love is a form of knowing, *knowing incompletely, wanting to know, dying to tell.* But maybe the only secret the lover cannot bear is whether the other loves one at all, and does the existence of the couple, the reference to "their" shared home, in which, on a wall, the two safes of 20-by-25-by-20 centimeters will hang, not imply some certainty on the matter of some quantity of love existing, so that this single basal question is in fact known and settled? *Will we dwell together?* At least this answer is yes.

It also assumes some other things.

Barthes

"*I like, I don't like*: this is of no importance to anyone; this, apparently, has no meaning. And yet all this means: *my body is not the same as yours*. Hence, in this anarchic foam of tastes and distastes, a kind of listless blur, gradually appears the figure of a bodily enigma, requiring complicity or irritation. Here begins the intimidation of the body, which obliges others to endure me *liberally*, to remain silent and polite confronted by pleasures or rejections which they do not share."[1]

A secret is a vacant form—paper street plan; fogged and wasted film. Secrets are MacGuffins, though we cannot be sure there are not lions in the Highlands. My secret attests only to this: *my body is not the same place as yours*. Respect the difference.

Contract

A selection of those contracts that may address lovers: the promissory ring, the I-love-you, the marriage, the dowry or mahr, the deed of shared property, the adoption certificate, the birth certificate, the mortgage, the joint account, the deed of sale, the prenuptial, formalized consent (blanket, suspended, meta-, non-), the divorce, power of attorney, the suicide pact, a will.

Sophie Calle's work does not require that its couple be married, but it does require that they form a natural couple, that they are in fact lovers, that they share a living space, are at least a *couple en concubinage*. Prior to entering the contract, therefore, the two parties have already participated in a number of agreements with each other, with property, and with language. Obviously, they are not strangers to each other. (A stranger's secret is often illegible. It is also often dull. [These are two risks Calle accepts for herself.]) The lovers, the ones with the secrets, have declared themselves a couple for fiscal or other purposes and have already thereby given up the status (and some rights) of those who are to be recognized as single. A status designated by a contract means that the parties are not free to determine the law for themselves. We have now arrived at the general question of any public interest in a private couple.

How is the work's Agreement like other contracts? It is at once a declaration of the existence of the couple, a document of ownership, and a deed of authentication articulating when the work is and is not a work of art. It is also some other things.

Secrets need the contract because they require defending. They are just so easy to wound. Easier than bodies. More like love. Drunk, I slip up; an error or nervous laugh; a tired relieving; omitting an omission; swapped and shuffled details. The work courts collapse; it is a simple thing to render it silly, superfluous, null, not a work of art at all but just two safes, one plaque, and a voided contract. Some paper, and a bit of metal.

In the formal parlance of Calle's corpus, the contract functions as the safe's caption. It converts things to photographs and in turn they contract it to explain (something); the contract forces the safes to be meaningful for awhile.

In "Le froid et le cruel," Gilles Deleuze emphasizes the degree to which "in his attempt to derive the law from the contract, the masochist aims not to mitigate the law but on the contrary to emphasize its extreme severity. For while the contract implies in principle certain conditions like the free acceptance of the parties, a limited duration and the preservation of inalienable rights, the law that it generates always tends to forget its own origins and annul these restrictive conditions. Thus the contract-law relationship involves in a sense a mystification … Since the law results in our enslavement, we should place enslavement first, as the dreadful object of the contract. One could even say, as a general rule, that in masochism the contract is caricatured in order to emphasize its ambiguous destination."[2] This contract is not very ambiguous. Three ontologies can undergo change: the lovers can break up (the couple destroyed); the work can no longer be declared to be a work of art (the artwork destroyed); or the artist can die, transferring responsibility to her representative (the living body destroyed). All three endings might well occur; at least one certainly will. I love the arrogance of a contract, insisting it can account for endings in advance. *If* they separate or divorce in the contract means *when* they separate or divorce. Lovers like bodies are provisional works.

After a certain upheaval in the history of contract law, a contract might be nullified because of mutual mistakes, voided because both parties did not consent to the same thing. This revision narrows the class of enforceable contracts, and means that arbiters are less interested in

meaning than in what the parties did—how they lived among their walls day after day. The law, as elsewhere, must go by externals, and judge parties by their conduct. No weight is given to states of mind.

The contract here is signed by Calle, each Owner, and the Artist's Representative. A signature is more than a name but less than the trace of the entire absent body. It is, at best, a mark made by the weight of the side of one hand, accompanied by a date specifying what has here and now as a one-time assent taken place. In this sense, it is like some secrets.

Destroy

Temptation to, I mean. As in the left foot of Michelangelo's *David*.

Calle's work proposes a new form of intimacy, the proof of which will be the vandalism and subsequent eradication of the artwork. The safes are not beautiful, but they are seductive. Put another way: the contract transforms love into the possibility of iconoclasm. Does this raise the stakes of love or lower them?

The work is a work of art, according to the strictures of the Agreement, solely under specific conditions. Stipulation 9: "If ever the Artist realises that one half of the Couple attempted to break in (physically or intellectually) or succeeded in obtaining the secret kept in the other half of the Couple's safe, the Work shall be inauthentic and no longer a work by the Artist. The same shall occur in the event of a break-in of the safe." No other situation—the death of the Artist, death of the Couple, sale of transfer, donation to a gallery—nullifies the Work as an authentic work of the Artist. Unaddressed is the thief's disappointment.

For no particular reason, one day it becomes unbearable to think that there are worlds of your lover you cannot access. This is the kind of conversation often had in the late afternoon, deliberately lingering amid snarls of sheets, the nape still damp, forearm wales not yet faded and we feel so close but how much closer might we feel, reaching out the plummy fruit *tell me yes, yes I want to tell you, I want you yes and yes this is a way to still be new together*.

If you were at this moment to measure blood volume and pulse amplitude, so recently subsided, there would be a noticeable autonomic increase.

But if these two lovers are to disunite secret and safe, the violation will come at a cost. Their profit will have ruined, irremediably, the work of art, any affective vitality mitigated, at least a bit, by the minutes later—for true secrets do not take long to say—as the sheets need be straightened, the children will be home soon, and someone needs to go grab a towel, and both are thinking now we are poorer, our assets diminished, all that capital wasted and nothing to show our friends, plus we will have to notify Sophie, I guess it's over, there's nothing else, I guess we take them off the wall now, and was it worth it, after all, after all, if one, drying the leg and smoothing the skirt should say, You know, I knew that all along. I knew that one, all along.

Lovers, strictly speaking, are conspirators. *Conspiratio*: lit. (merely) to breathe together.

Eroticism

[s.v. "obedience," see **Contract**]

Frustration

—I have forgotten my secret. Honestly. I have forgotten my password, my answer, my wallet, my promise, my place, details of some old lies.

Grammar

Examples of conditional sentences include: *If she fell, she would get hurt. If he had asked her to be with him, she would have blown up her world. If it rains, I will get wet.* Type two conditionals refer to a hypothetical condition and its probable results, but the temporality is shifted to the present and its consequences in the real are implied: *If you really had loved me, you would have said so at the time. (But you didn't, and so you never did.) If the rain had not started, we would have taken a walk. (But it is pouring, thus we will not go.)* It is appropriate to use the subjunctive mood and write, for example, *If I were sure that you really wanted me, I would be able to come (but I am not, and accordingly stay shy).* Or, *If I were a flower, I would crave the rain.* A lover's

secret may take a conditional tense (*If my father had cut me off, I would have broken our engagement*, or *If you had not lost the baby, I would have left you both*), but of course it does not have to: e.g., the present perfect continuous is well suited for stating *I have been puking after dinner for the last three years.* The conditional does not name certainties. *I will get older, and I will regret having left you*; *I will regret we never spent the night together*; *I will regret all the days apart* are not optimal terms for a conditional sentence. *Now can you say whether you loved me, now that your attention is elsewhere?* is also not hypothetical. A rather excitingly "mixed type" of construction specifies the results in the present of an unreal past condition: If + Past Perfect – Would + Inf. For example: *If you had told me (then), I would not be so suspicious (now). If you had warned me (then), I would not still be holding out hope ([cruelly] now).*

All lovers' secrets can be translated into one specific conditional verb form: *If you knew X, you would no longer love me (as much, at all, the same, again).* The content of this declaration is less important than the formalism of a perceived threat to love (because it induces shame, because it suggests fault, it trivializes, recasts histories, maybe it cheapens or else compromises, tarnishes or bruises).

Grammarians regard the conditional as ideal for specifying an unreal, improbable, even impossible situation. Yet rain, never having been loved, and falling all seem real, possible, even probable.

How to evade certain of these conditions

>You can always burn your shared house
>and thus each of your shared walls
>to the ground.
>(Acquire new shelter.)

>Undertake to seduce
>the Artist (or her representative) and at a later time
>propose, as a gesture of an ardent love—you only
>>require one person
>to endure censure and disregard
>the law
>and betray the rules of the work
>for you.

In the Mood for Love

I once fell in love with someone. Usually secrets begin this way. *I couldn't stop wondering if she loved me back.* Though some begin this way.

I didn't think it would hurt so much.

Not every secret is kept in the same way. The way is what matters.

Some end with: *Then let me tell you something.* (Others begin this way.)

In the old days, he says, *if someone had a secret they didn't want to share, you know what they did? They went up a mountain, found a tree, carved a hole in it, and whispered the secret into the hole. Then they covered it with mud, leaving the secret there forever.*

One the monk at the temple; two the hole, the grazing finger; three his profile and the ridges of rock—and when he leans in, his cheek disappears, absorbed into the texture of stone—four the spectral encircling of columns. Leaving him to the long, jaw-tremoring whisper, the camera turns away, this drift of the image giving a measure of privacy. Also the jarring orange; also the impossibly high angle and magisterial space; also the green, the blue, the hallway and light-split stairs, the earth, the grassy earth spilling out, blocking and filling what once was a hole that ruining time, and not the lover, had initially carved.

Jealous

It would be neither incorrect nor unusual to say of someone that he or she has guarded a secret *jealously*.

In the preceding usage, what, precisely, does the last word mean?

Kindnesses

Only have told me secrets: a mule's burden of words, and dragging now.
Never have told me secrets, claiming at a gray-eyed distance to have none.

Last two lines of a villanelle

How do you know that I happened to you?
Love is what you do not do.

Midas

It seems an overreaction when, in response to the king's awarding the victory, in response to the beautiful music, in response to the competition—the Pan-Apollo stuff—his ears are stretched and lengthened, weakened, and probably wounded—while it is not specified how or if they tore, at some point in being stretched skin becomes too thin not to fray and the elasticity (especially if it is quick, and we have no reason to presume patience) weakens and fails, gives way—no sense of how long it took to heal, and obviously amateurish or hurried stretching can lead to infection, to scarring (nor is it reported what, if anything, this did to his sense of balance)—and after all someone had to win: this seems unfair as they did demand the contest be judged and he did only what was asked. The king arranges his hair differently. He thinks it hides the ruined pinnae. This leaves only the problem of the barber. (Artist will have to learn from him.) On this point, the reports diverge: it is said the king pleaded with the man, but it is also said the king ordered the man. One pleads from those in the face of whom one has no power; one orders those over whom one has entire power. Either way, the message was: This ugly's what you must not tell. Here once more our accounts disagree on the details: some are rather hard on the barber, insist he was unable, unwilling even, to honor the juicy oath. But one can also err by being overly charitable: a few versions tack maudlin, make the king's story into one of the haircutter's illness, emphasize the weight of the secret, its toll on *his* spirit, *his* visceral, emetic need to cast it out. Either way, on this agreement they are willing to end: barber digs a hole and sets his mouth in the mud and looses—then he grabs enough dirt, pats the depression, smooths the ground, and gets on with it. In some versions, it is a tree that grows and divulges the gossip to animals who spread it abroad. But in most, reeds flourish on that patch of scarred land, and the wind, slattern cunt, makes them spill the defacement over and over for all to hear.

In his youth, offered love, the king instead asks to have everything he touch turn to gold.

Later, he begs for the gift to be taken away.

Nothing

Calle's rules ensure that nothing is not a possible outcome; this game cannot end in a draw. One is not permitted to declare *I have no secrets*, no coy *that is my secret*. Nor may one party demur, raise doubts, abstain in protest. Silence, blankness, reticence, and above all asymmetry are thereby curtailed. This is a kind of fairness.

Open

Containing secrets, the safes are closed. Empty, they remain open. Slightly parted, not unlike stunned or hungry mouths, would it be preferable to write of these doors that they are *ajar* or that they are *agape*?

Agapē is an interesting word for lovers because it is the love they do not do; neither *eros* (*I want to clean you like a cat, with my tongue*) nor *philia* (which Aristotle gives as "wanting for someone what one thinks good, for his sake and not for one's own, and being inclined, as far as one can, to do such things for him"[3]—*It has been a bad year and I am broken*; the friend, *iff* said with no intent to seduce, replies: *I want to unbreak you*), Christian *agape* is the unconditional love, that of God and charity, compassion, radical forgiveness (as in Kierkegaard's agapeistic ethics: principled, transcendental, abstract, what Adorno dubs "cruel" in its cool rigor). Before then, in ancient literature, it named numerous forms of affection, including loving one's child and loving the dead, and sometimes, presumably, and economically, those loves overlapped. The agape mouth dates to the seventeenth century, at which point affection is converted into wonder. The etymologies, however, have nothing in common; what gapes is a breach, an opening in a wall, unfilled space, and has more in common (despite the wonderment) with the Old English *ginian* for yawn.

Ajar: what is neither open nor shut.

So either term will do.

Psychoanalysis

"That the dream actually has a secret meaning, which turns out to be the fulfillment of a wish, must be proved afresh for every case by means of an analysis. I therefore select several dreams which have painful contents and attempt an analysis of them. They are partly dreams of hysterical subjects, which require long preliminary statements, and now and then also an examination of the psychic processes which occur in hysteria. I cannot, however, avoid this added difficulty in the exposition."[4]

Questions

For example, what happens between steps two and four as outlined in the plaque? Each half of the couple is to tell this artist a secret. Each secret is to be locked up in its own safe. But let us presume some time passes as the safes are being installed—let's not get distracted by the noise and studs, the levels and sensors, cutting the holes and worrying over wiring—and instead ask: what all the while is happening with those now-told secrets? This is where the crookedness of the game appears. Things are no longer adding up; I suspect other scenes. For there is an unstated leap between "Have each of them tell me a secret" and "Lock each secret up in its own safe."

How is the secret to be told to the Artist (whispered, in person, in French, all at once, over a dozen agonizing negotiations—is she priest or translator, student or scribe)? How, affectively, is the secret thus confessed (with delight, in heat—she is at least requesting this intimacy, no torture room like the receipt of unwanted confidence—or with footnotes and alibis, defenses, or just flatly)? Does Calle then write it down right away, jot a mnemonic, remember it easily? Are the two secrets told in sequence, on different days, and who goes first, and who decided who goes first, and what if there is tension about how it was decided who would get to go first? And what happens now (always the question)? By the time the safes are finally firmly installed, at the "Lock each secret up in its own safe" stage, what form has the secret taken? Has she written it in ink or pencil, in cursive or plain, or is the secret typed, and in what face, and has she rephrased, paraphrased, annotated it, or is it verbatim, transcribed meticulously, and what has thereby been lost— or what has thereby been gained? The details, obviously, matter—one detail otherwise and I might have been able to tell you, we might have shared a laugh over the whole episode. And how are the pronouns to be handled: in uttering the secret, presumably there has been an *I*, and has she retained it or has each *I* become its avatar, discourse directed into a "He" who "said" some "that" that "he," et cetera. What if Calle forgets—there are other projects, after all, and trains to catch, and life does not stop because two lovers have secrets—or, when the wordings become confused: are there provisions for clarification? We still have not yet begun to treat the enormous matter of punctuation, including but not limited to those designating terminus, emphasis, enthusiasm, irony. All this is the secret of the work. Or, rather, it appears to be so until one turns to the contract.

For in the Letter of Agreement that constitutes the final part of the four-part work—two safes, one accompanying plaque, these three to be installed on the wall in the home, and now also this, the contract (which is shown with the provisional work but presumably, being a legal document of some import, will find itself, at the moment the safes are themselves installed, the secrets therein, copied and placed in its own safe, in a bank or in the closet, at the new distance demanded by living in the wake of the game [It is exhilarating to tell someone new something new, but in time they have heard it all before, or at least are not someone new, and eventually the safes will have to be dusted, and who will dust the safes will not itself remain a secret, and the codes for the other safe, the one with the copy of the contract, plus maybe the gallery documentation, lost then found then lost again . . .])—in the second sentence already is the first discrepancy. "Each safe must contain a secret in an envelope or other container given to Sophie Calle (the 'Artist') by each person representing one half of the Couple. Neither half of the Couple has or shall have access to the secret of the other. The Artist undertakes not to disclose the secrets."

Let us pause here. All of a sudden, we are dealing with envelopes. Instead of the couple telling Calle their secrets, they each hand over an object and now unspecified is whether it must only contain words or whether words can or will be accompanied by an image—supplanted, even, by an image, or some thing, or a thing or an image on which has been written something else, and then which element constitutes the secret, precisely? And are the envelopes to be left unsealed, later closed by the Artist, mouth to the gum, her saliva staining the edge of the paper, or does she prefer wax or glue or tape? Or are they given over already sealed, to be

ripped open and exhumed by the Artist, and once more we have questions of duration, protocol, handling—and are they produced at the same time, in each other's company, and if B were to see that A>B, by this I mean in terms of envelope dimension, thickness, weight, for whom might this discrepancy in volume enclosing confession become a new, and fully known, source of turmoil—and we have still not yet answered the prior queries regarding protocols for sealing (now resealing), which present themselves once more and remain unclarified.

There are fundamental differences between the plaque and the contract. I am not trying to be mean; I am aiming for precision. But how could the Agreement be precise enough? No contract can account for every contingency, which is why arbitration, to take place only in written form, is provided in the final stipulation. Unsaid is what becomes of that writing. The contract only allows nomination, transferal, or destruction. Unsteady negotiation. There will not be an end to questioning.

These strict and noisy instructions: they guarantee nothing. Let us never hold this against the effort.

What can you take? *Can you take me having the secret but no one knowing, can you take someone knowing but not you, can you take knowing who knows but it not being you, can you take seeing the envelope, can you take feeling its weight, can you take making out lines of script upon holding its plane to the light, can you take wondering if I lied, can you take wondering if I did not lie (why didn't I sense it is both a question and an accusation), could you ever call a bluff, can you take putting the thing in the safe yourself, can you take the closing of the chest, can you take seeing me smirk or finding it all quite light, can you take me chiding you for not deeming it amusing, can you take seeing me take your secret with ease, can you take wondering for whom love is always lovely, can you take sensing me not give a damn about your secret, can you take me suggesting your secret is likely tame (ridiculous even), can you see me unbothered by someone knowing but not me?*

Lover asks two questions: How much can you bear, and will you accept (believe) the apology (remorse)?

My entire history of falling short.
—But we laughed every day.

Rules

Find a couple.
Have each of them tell me a secret.
Install two safes in their home.
Lock each secret up in its own safe.
Keep the codes to myself.
The lovers will have to live with the other's secret
close at hand but out of reach.

Separation

If words are to be trusted, a secret is a separation. Perhaps in stating a secret each lover gets to announce that they are ultimately on their own. *We have excluded each other at least one time.* The Latin *secretus*, what is hidden or concealed or private—the veiled quality most familiar to us—is a form of the more interesting *secernere*, "to set or put apart," "to place asunder," "to divide," even "to sever." *Cernere*, "to sift or distinguish"; also "to decide."

I have distinguished my body from yours. I already wrote this decision, we have not moved on.

Safes also separate in that they hold valuables *en sauf*, in safety, free from—excluded, marked distinct from—danger; uninjured, protected, and watched over (earlier forms imply both assured spiritual salvation and the earthier good, solid health); intact; cloistered from all risk, save, of course, the risk each safe solicits: that of being robbed. Safes also, in taking in and absorbing the secrets, holding them outside economies whereby they might be deployed (the secret kept truly safe must never be *used*), could be said to consume the secret, as in *consumptio, consumere*, "to use up, eat, deplete." Most safes resist the action of heat. Professional burglars speaking against self-interest recommend against safes with thin metal doors, in addition to those bolted only to the wall. They are easy to remove in full, to be interfered with elsewhere at a later time.

Trust

Calle here takes on the opposite role of the Barthesian *l'Informateur* in *Fragments d'un discours amoureaux*—the one in the public amative network who "busies himself and *tells everyone everything*." This informer, Barthes specifies, "by furnishing me insignificant information about the one I love . . . discovers a secret for me. This secret is not a deep one, but comes from outside: it is the other's 'outside' which was hidden from me. The curtain rises the wrong way round—not on an intimate stage, but on the crowded theater. Whatever it tells me, the information is painful: a dull, ungrateful fragment of reality lands on me."[5] Instead, Calle will absorb the two secrets: house in her body the pressure of those inside confessions. Though, perhaps, at some cost. Who would not be delighted to receive in detail whispered words like *wrists, restraints, Damaris, inversion,* and who would remain unstained by slack confessions of cruelties against a childhood pet, or unbothered hearing of debts unsuspected by those whose encumbrance they will bear as inheritance? Who would not be mildly embarrassed to receive as the secret worthy of vaulting a carnal fascination one tired of decades earlier?

Secrets are aesthetic, in that they are oriented toward their judgment. Hidden, because they are judged in the negative. Exposed, because they are judged unbearable or illuminating, essential or urgent. A secondary humiliation is thus always possible: to utter, finally, one's secret and to be thusly responded: *And so?* One's secrets are above all one's own—one's improper property. To fail to be shocked is to fail to register the other as able to possess meaningful property. Those who cannot hold property also often may not enter into contracts.

Calle's work is constantly said to expose the innermost, to revel in the previously private (how others are unseeable to themselves, in torpor, possessions, habits [*The Sleepers*, 1980; *The Hotel*, 1981; *Cash Machine*, 1991–2003]; impersonal words to end the affair [*Take Care of Yourself*, 2007]; memories of suffering or the lived dying time of a mother [*Douleur Exquise*, 2003; *Rachel, Monique*, 2006]); but here she becomes the secret's cloister, its guarantor. *Share my bed* is not the same as *tell me. I will make your last milky sight* is not the same charge as *your secret is safe with me.* The function of the work is not to create the secret, but to prevent its easy obliteration (it is the future that requires the antithanatotic). *How do I know it was real unless someone else saw, knew, knows . . .* She gives this gift.

Unsure

The history of safes includes secrets hidden between the inner lining and outer wall. How can you be sure you are not living with her secrets, as well? It might not be a one-sided intimacy. To be sure, one would have to risk ruining everything.

Vanity

Doubtless, I would think it's about me.

Wearing one's heart on one's sleeve

It is very difficult for some people to keep secrets—others cannot help but perceive their inmost feelings. This is often cause for blushing. This is sometimes cause for disaster. Or one might offer up this disintegration of secrecy as proof of love. A lover's sleeve might have had pinned to it for general attention the favor of a lady. Harm is likely. Early in *Othello*, Iago vows, "I will wear my heart upon my sleeve for daws to peck at." Daws are small birds said to be foolish, worthless, and thievish.

"In the expression *wear one's heart on one's sleeve*, the verb functions as a trivalent predictor in a manner no different from its function in the non-idiomatic *wear one's name tag on one's lapel*; the third valence slot is in each case filled by a complement which is realized as an adverbial prepositional phrase with a regular and semantically motivated choice of preposition," instructs Ernst-August Müller in an essay on "Valence and Phraseology in Stratificational Linguistics."[6] This introduces a key question: will the two safes be labeled, one name tag placed on each? How do I know which secret I am looking at years later hanging on the wall? How can I be sure I would not risk breach only to find my own words spilled back to me?

X'd out

Lovers are waiting to no longer love. Someone leaves this work; it cannot just go on. This is what is declared *agreeable* in the Agreement.

There are only two events available to lovers: parting or death. So really, one.

You

Being what I have to live with.
Being what I cannot shake.

Zeroing in

How to maintain intact and in perpetuity?
Bodies are such sad stuff. Pinched nerves and thinning hair.

All along, we thought it was about love. But these are nothing but rules to be followed in the event of a death. "In case of the death of the Artist." The Agreement, what bonds the lovers to Calle in a curious and conscripted intimacy, is also a will, a document for the dispossession of the work *after*. It may be their secrets, but it is not not about her.

Assumptions

It assumes that there are lovers.
It assumes that some lovers have secrets.
It assumes that those secrets can be put into words.
It also assumes some other things.

Notes

[1] Roland Barthes, *Roland Barthes par Roland Barthes* [Roland Barthes by Roland Barthes], trans. Richard Howard (New York: Farrar, Straus and Giroux, 1977 [1975]).

[2] Deleuze, "Le froid et le cruel" [Coldness and Cruelty], in Deleuze and Leopold von Sacher-Masoch, *Masochism,* trans. Jean McNeil (New York: Zone Books, 1989 [1967]).

[3] Aristotle, *Rhetoric*, in *The Basic Works of Aristotle*, trans. W. D. Ross, ed. Richard McKeon (New York: Random House, 1941).

[4] Sigmund Freud, *Die Traumdeutung* [The Interpretation of Dreams], *The standard edition of the complete psychological works of Sigmund Freud*, vols. 4 and 5, ed. James Strachey (London: Hogarth Press, 1956–74 [1900]).

[5] Roland Barthes, *Fragments d'un discours amoureaux* [A Lover's Discourse: Fragments], trans. Richard Howard (New York: Noonday Press, 1978 [1977]).

[6] Müller, "Valence and Phraseology in Stratificational Linguistics," in *Functional Approaches to Language, Culture, and Cognition: Papers in Honor of Sydney M. Lamb,* ed. James E. Copeland, Peter H. Fries, and David G. Lockwood (Amsterdam: John Benjamins Publishing Co., 2000).

Plates

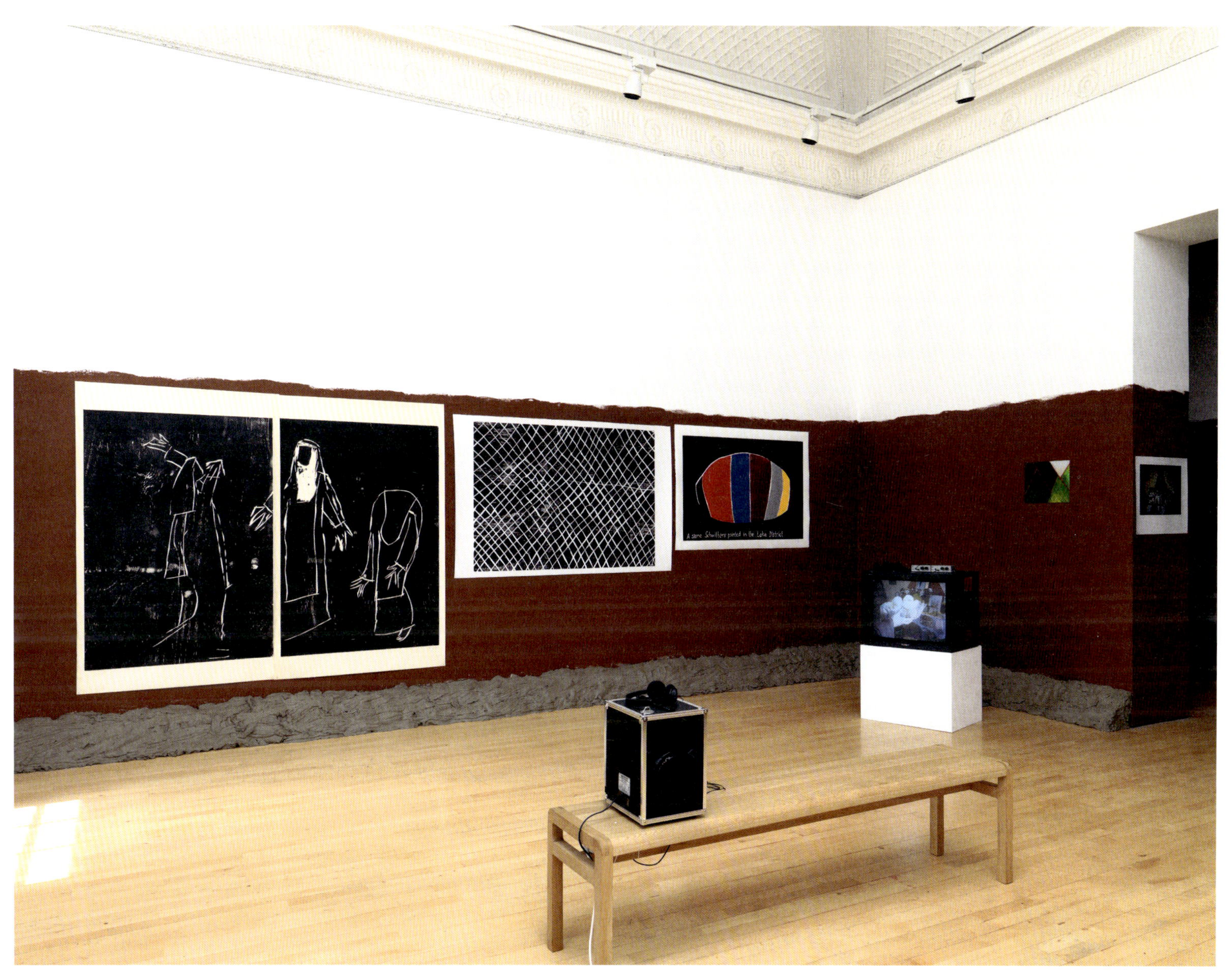

Brown Wall Painting, 2006

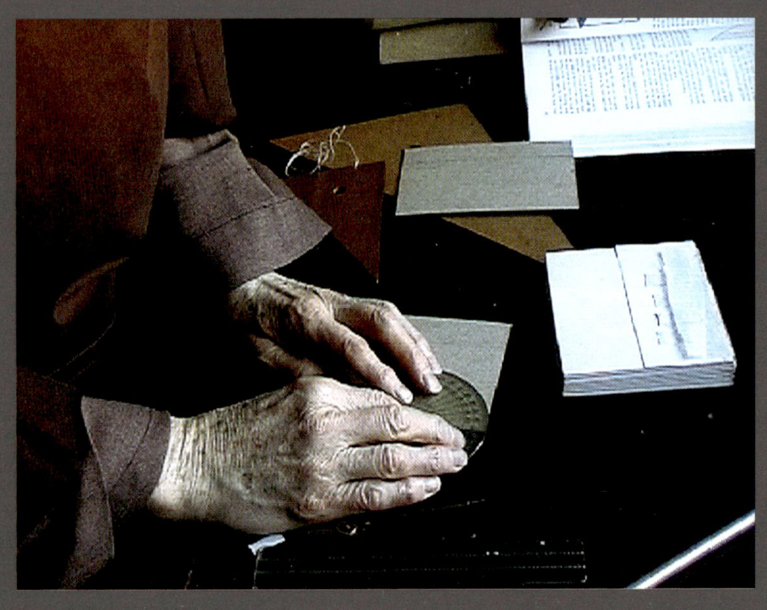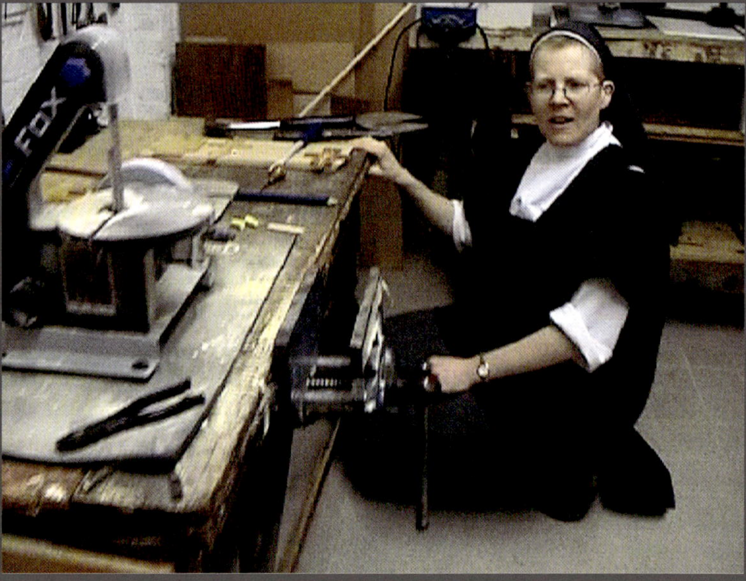

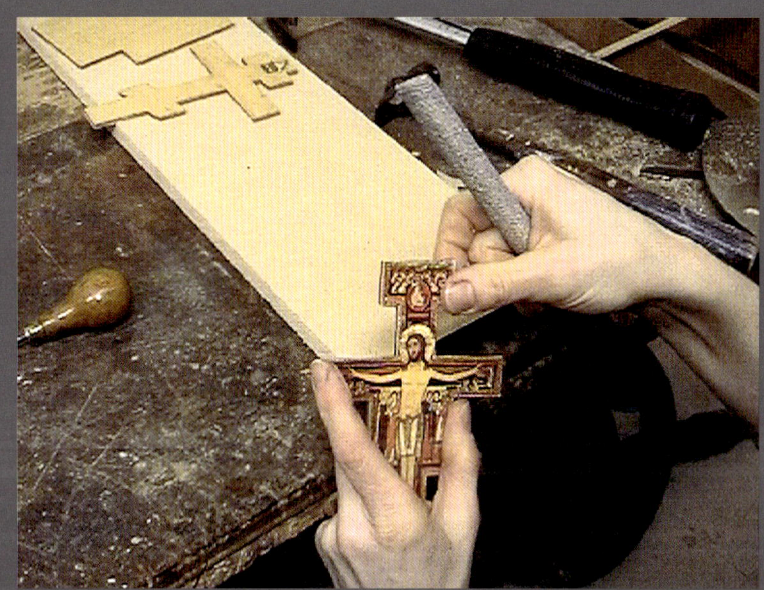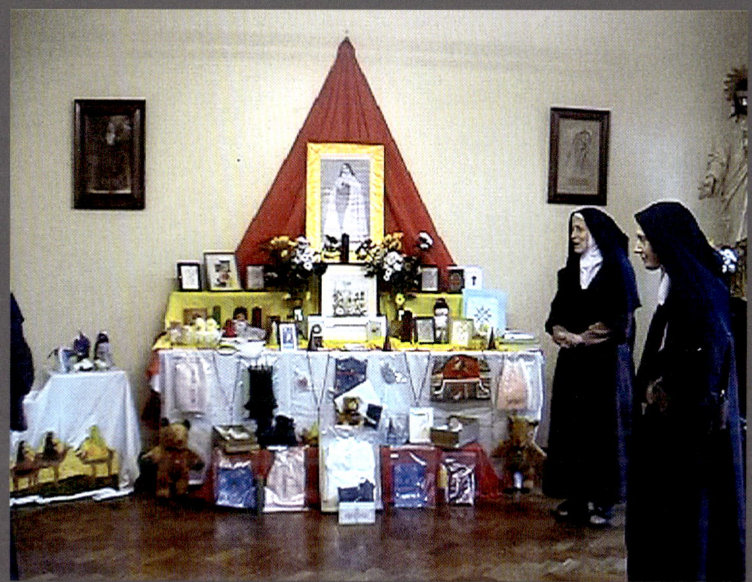

Little Works, 2007

SOPHIE CALLE

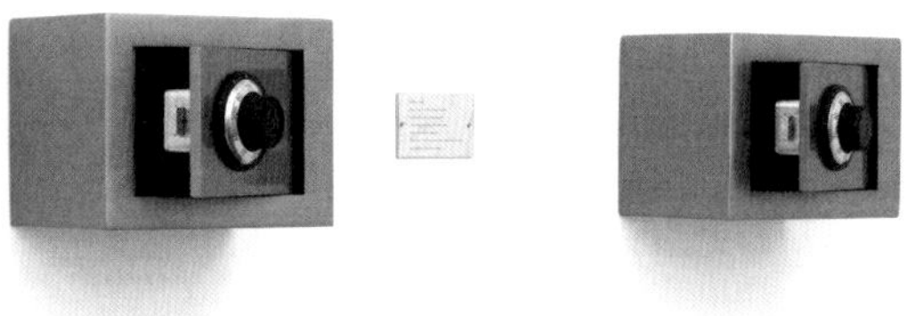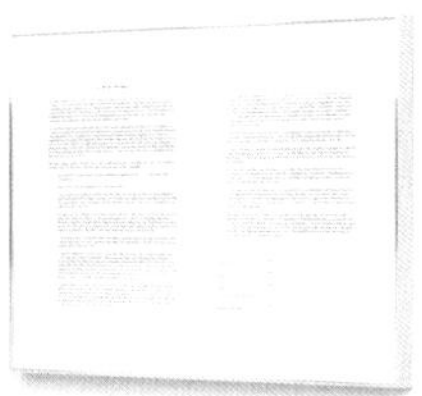

Secrets, 2014

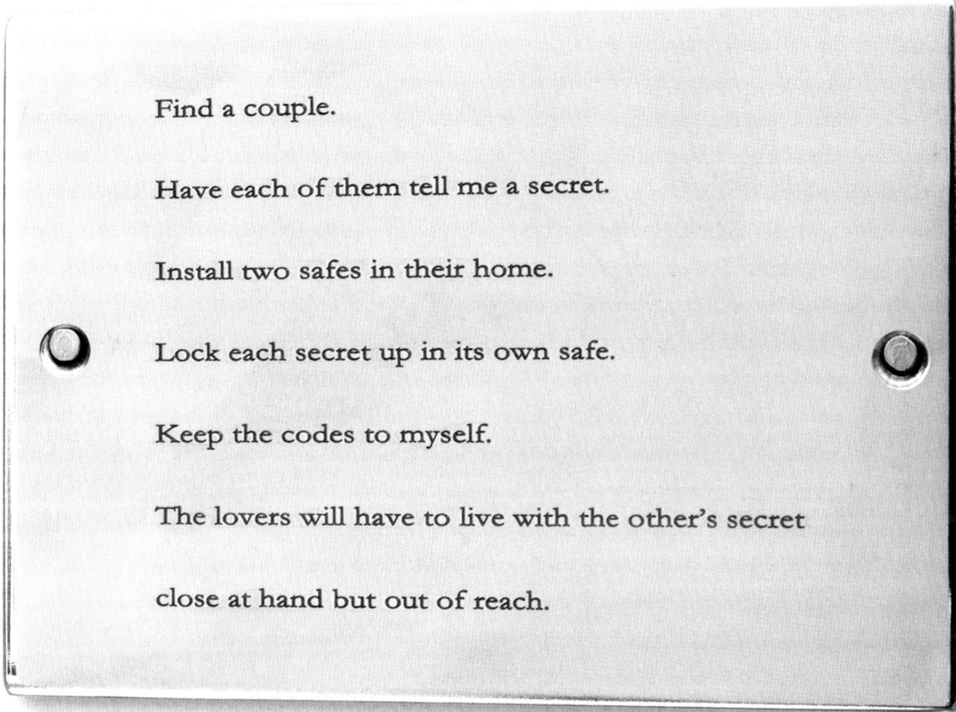

Find a couple.

Have each of them tell me a secret.

Install two safes in their home.

Lock each secret up in its own safe.

Keep the codes to myself.

The lovers will have to live with the other's secret

close at hand but out of reach.

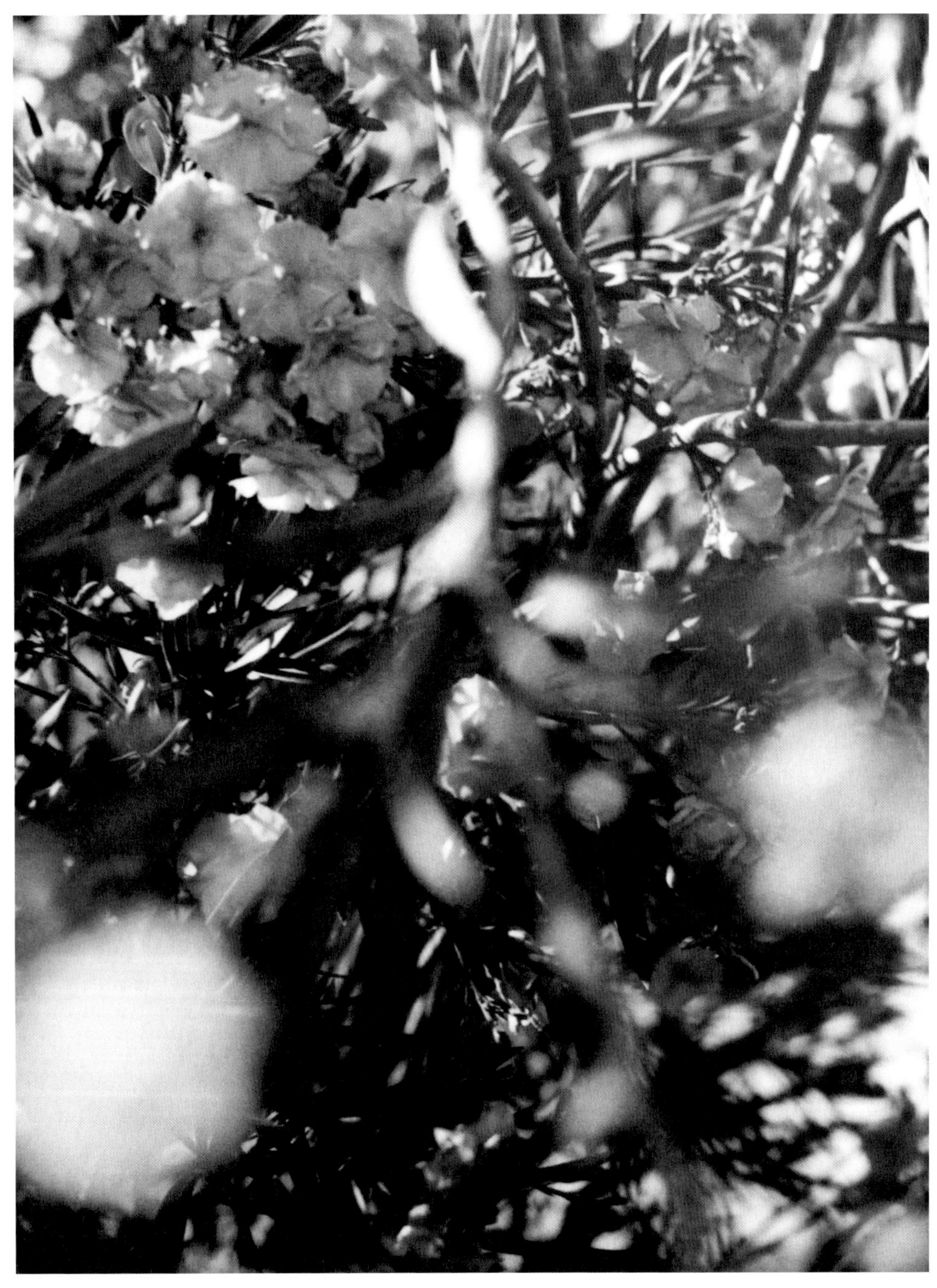

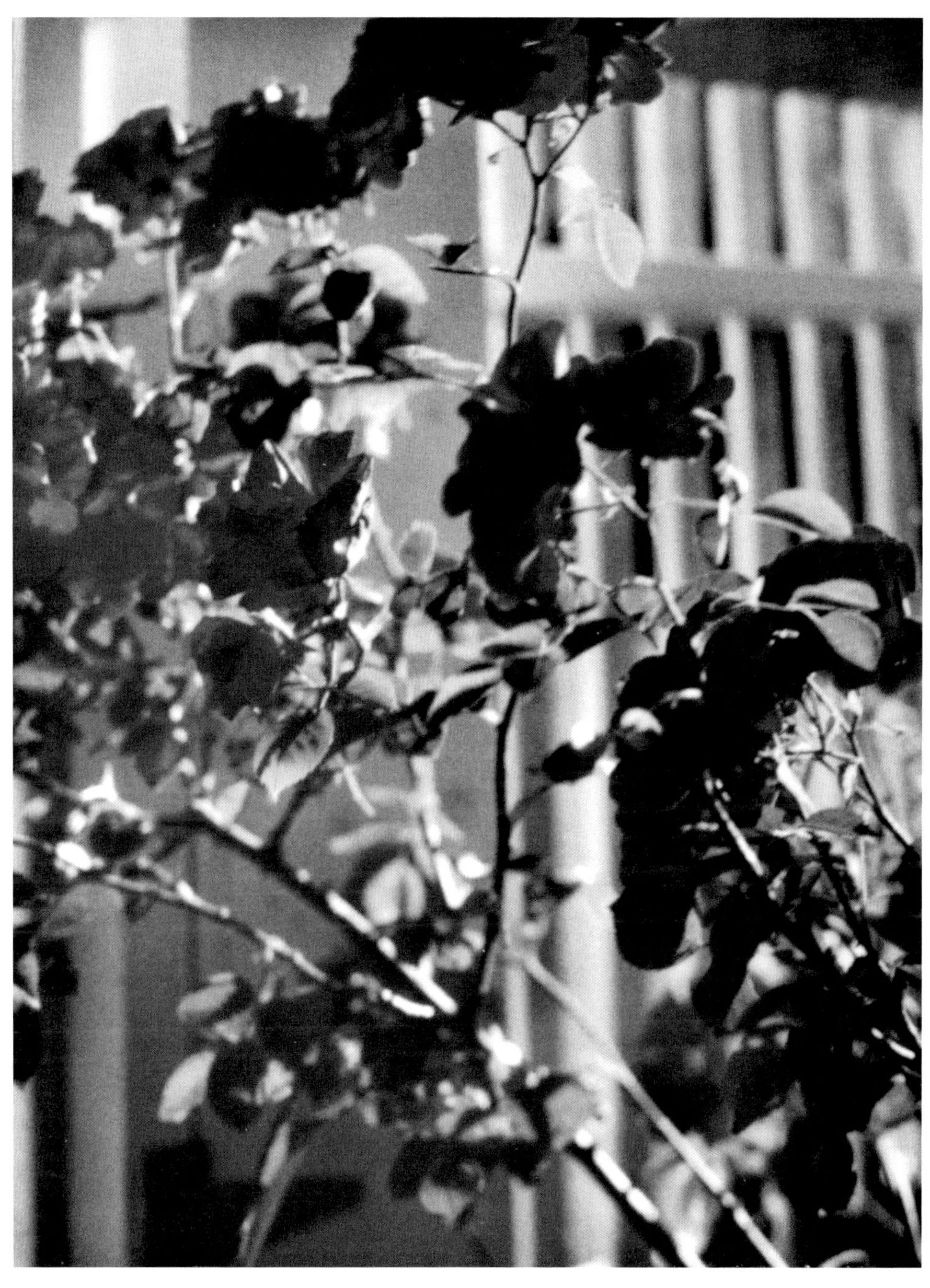

Fragile Images That Keep Producing Death While Attempting to Preserve Life:
Flowers found in crime scenes_001–004, 2011

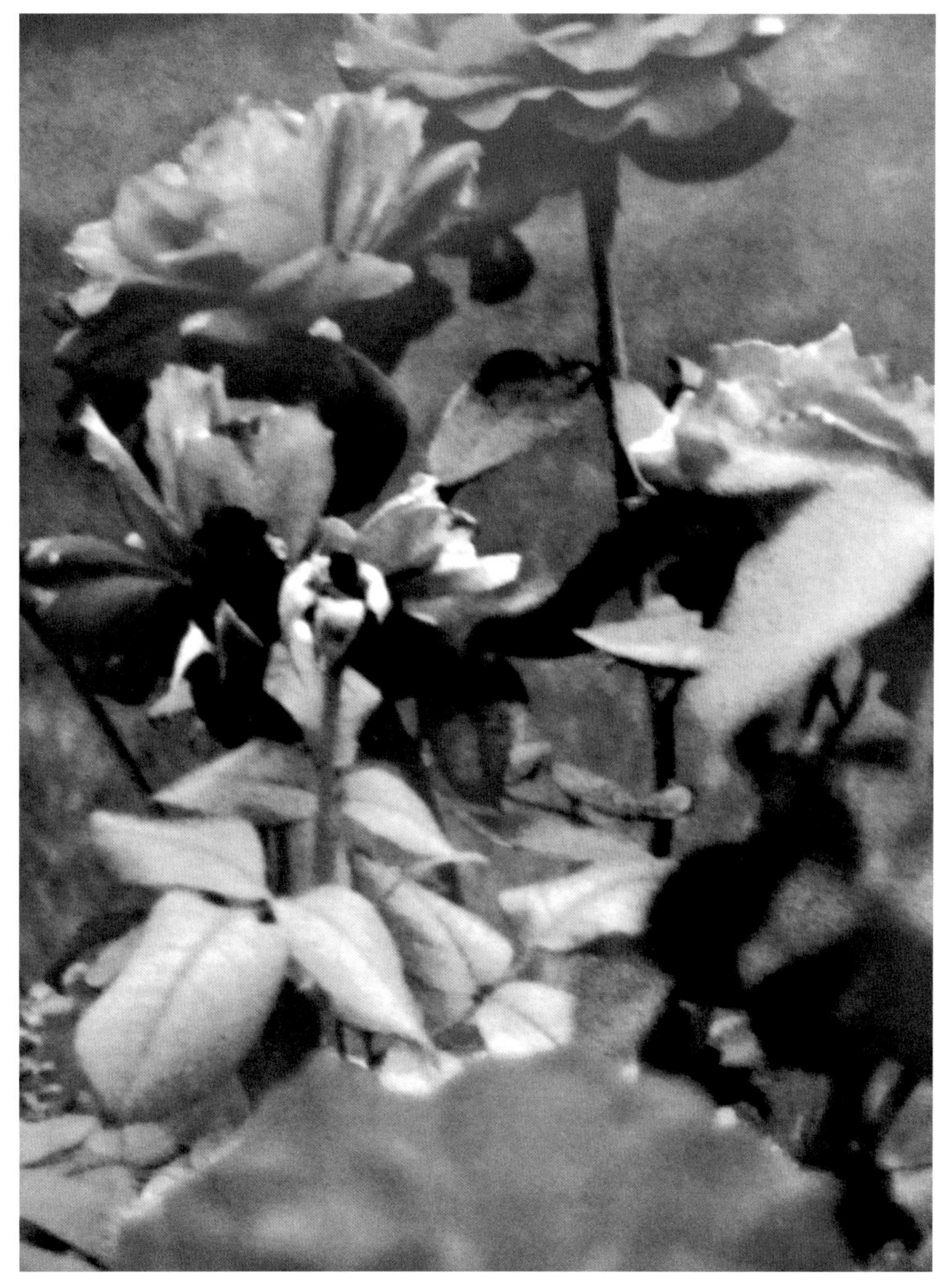

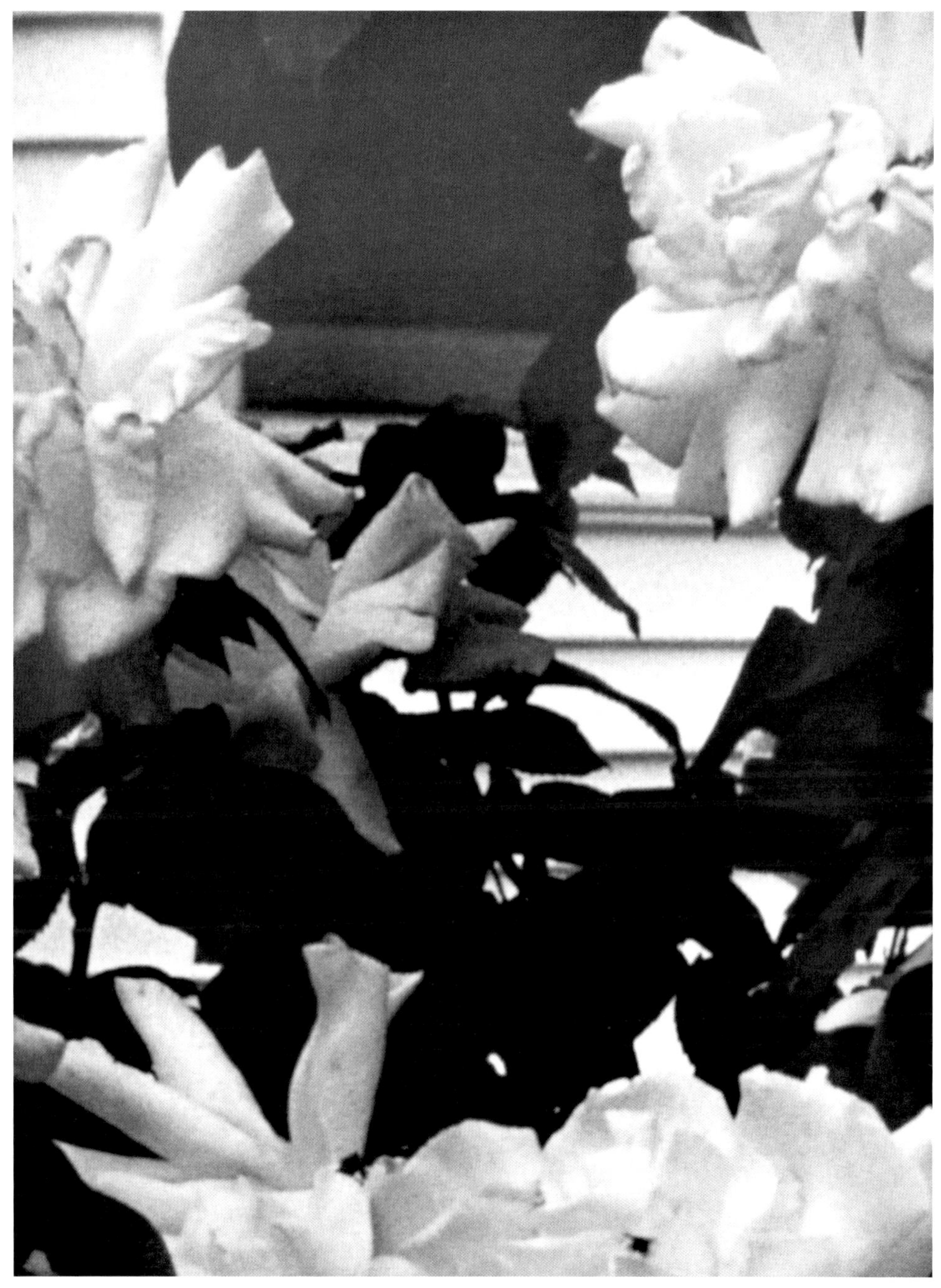

JASON DODGE

JASON DODGE

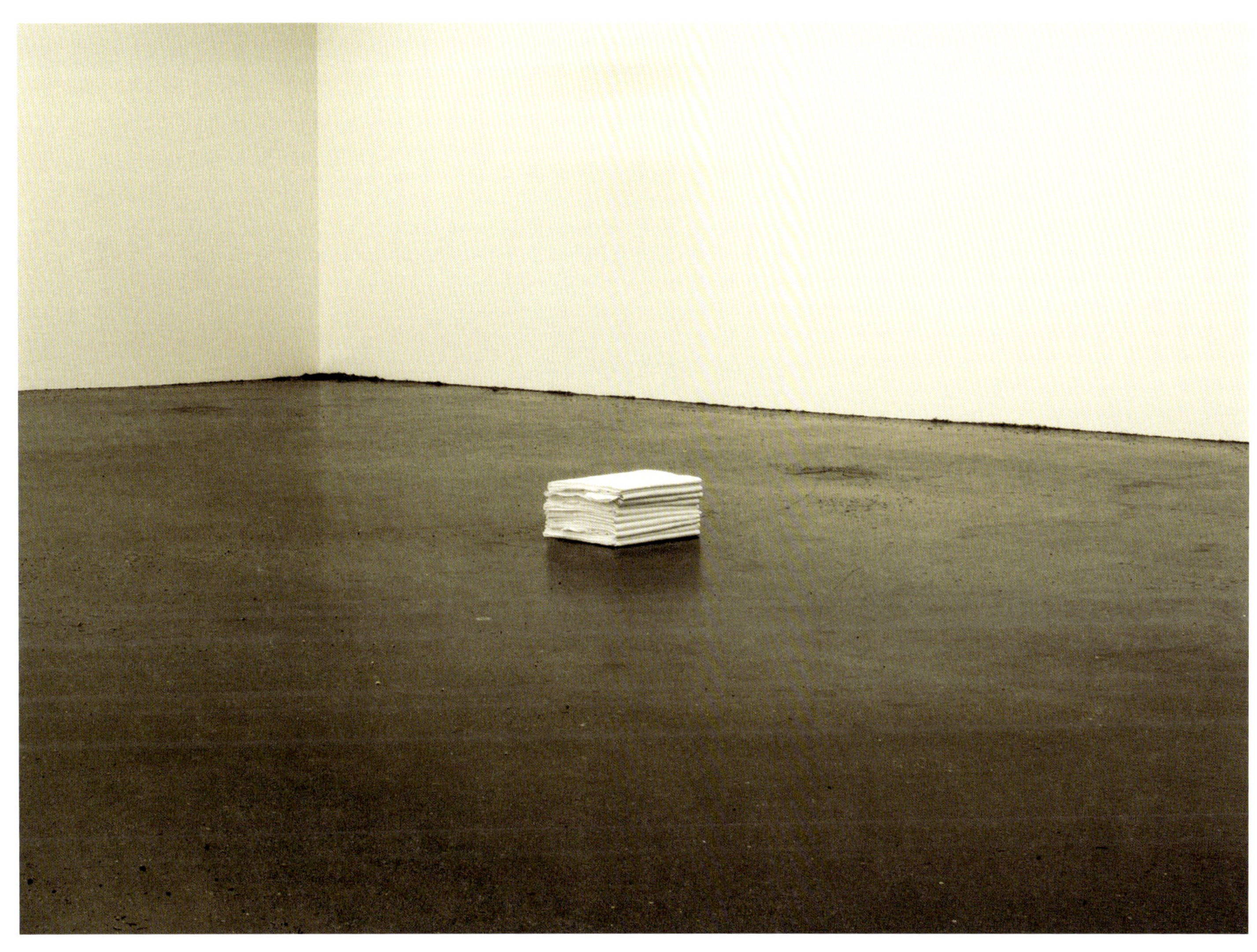

Anyone

FELIX GONZALEZ-TORRES

54

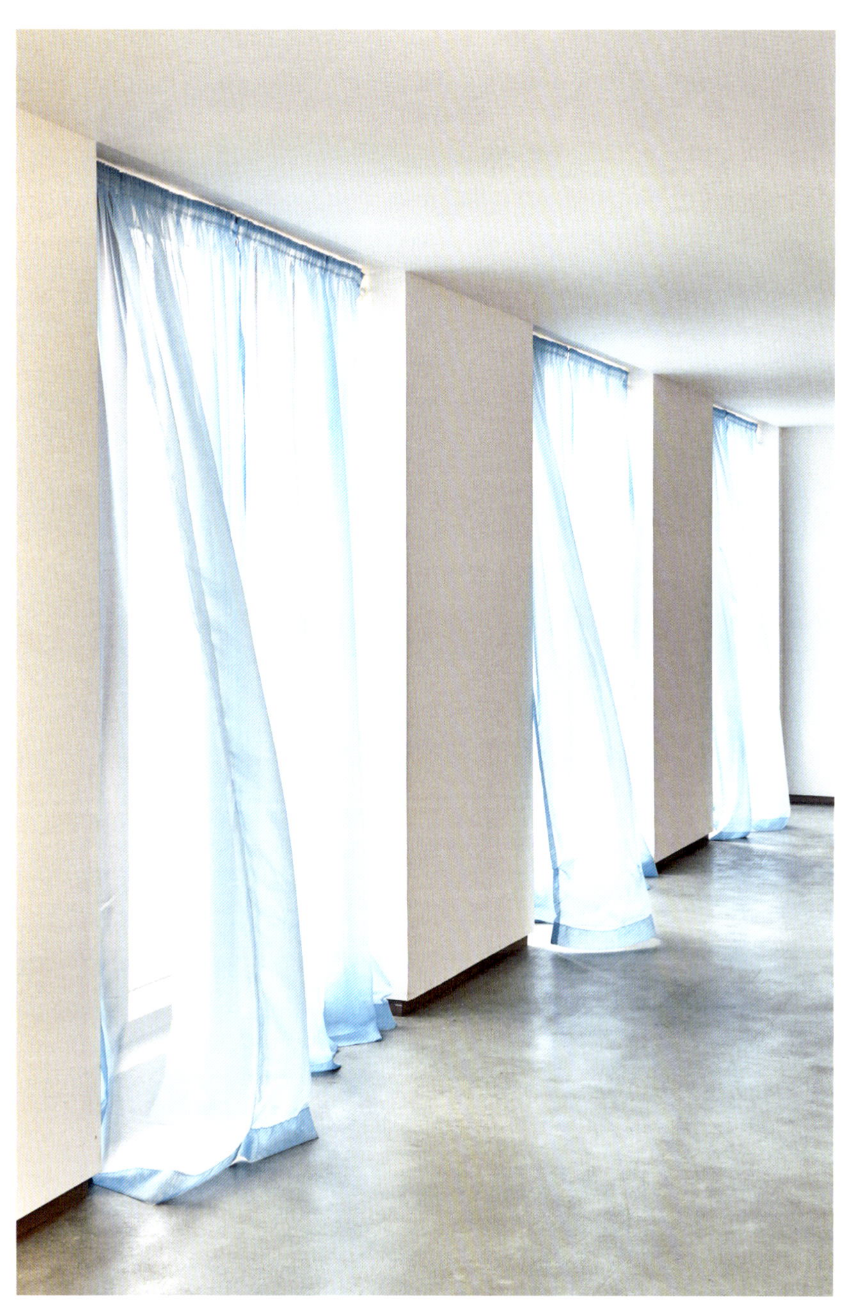

"Untitled" (Loverboy), 1989

56

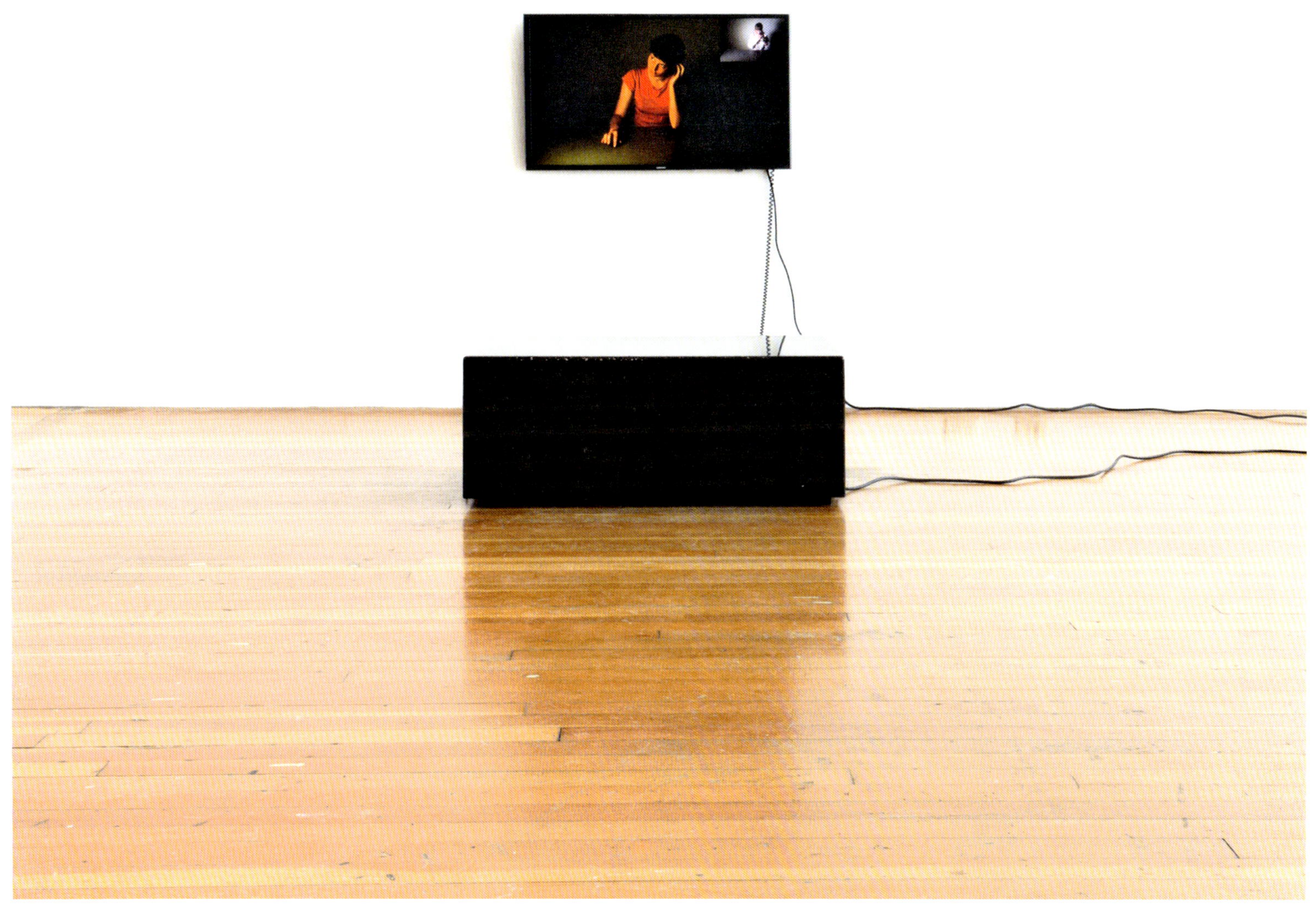

Object T, 2015

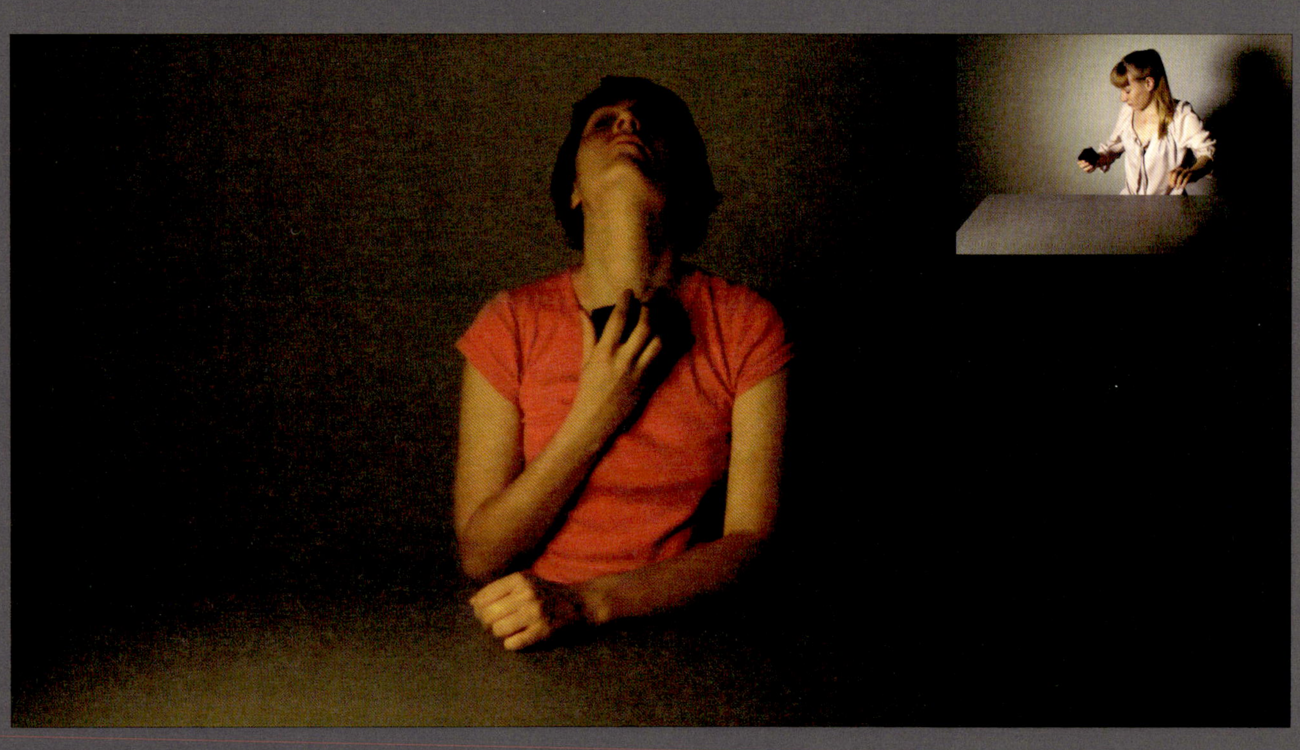

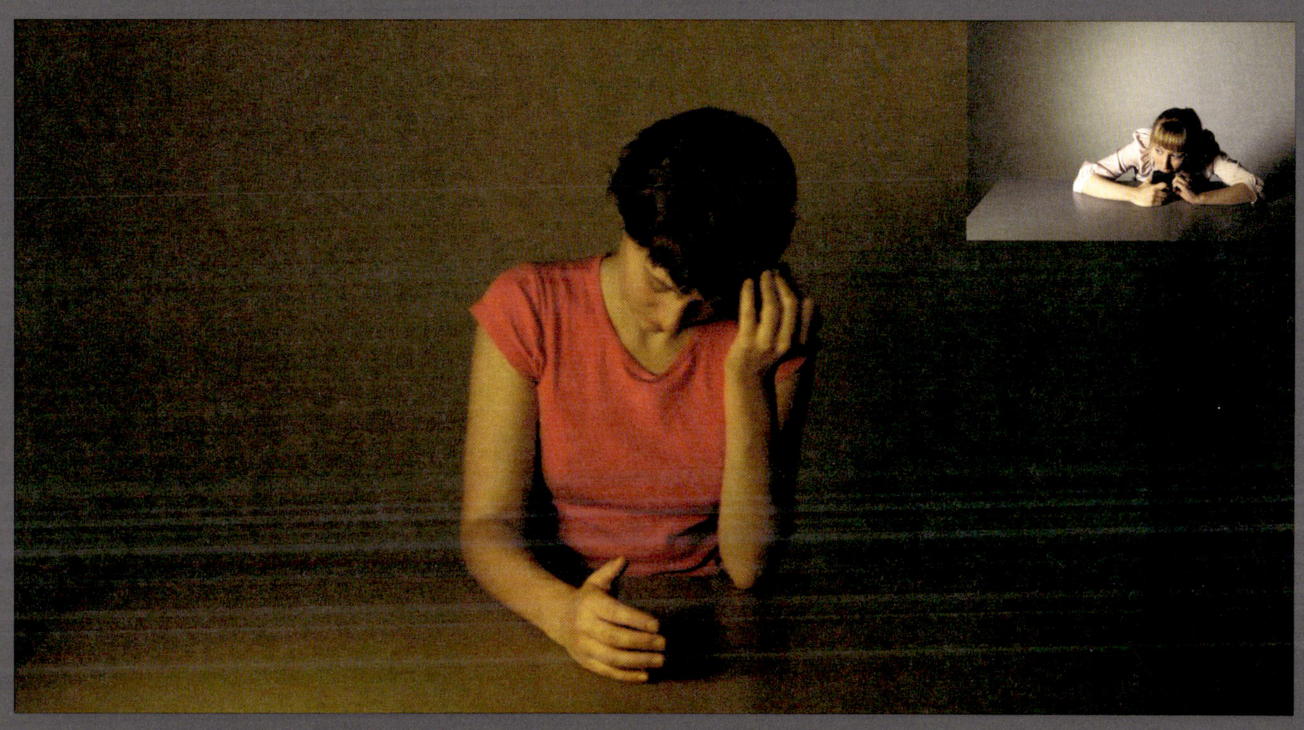

60

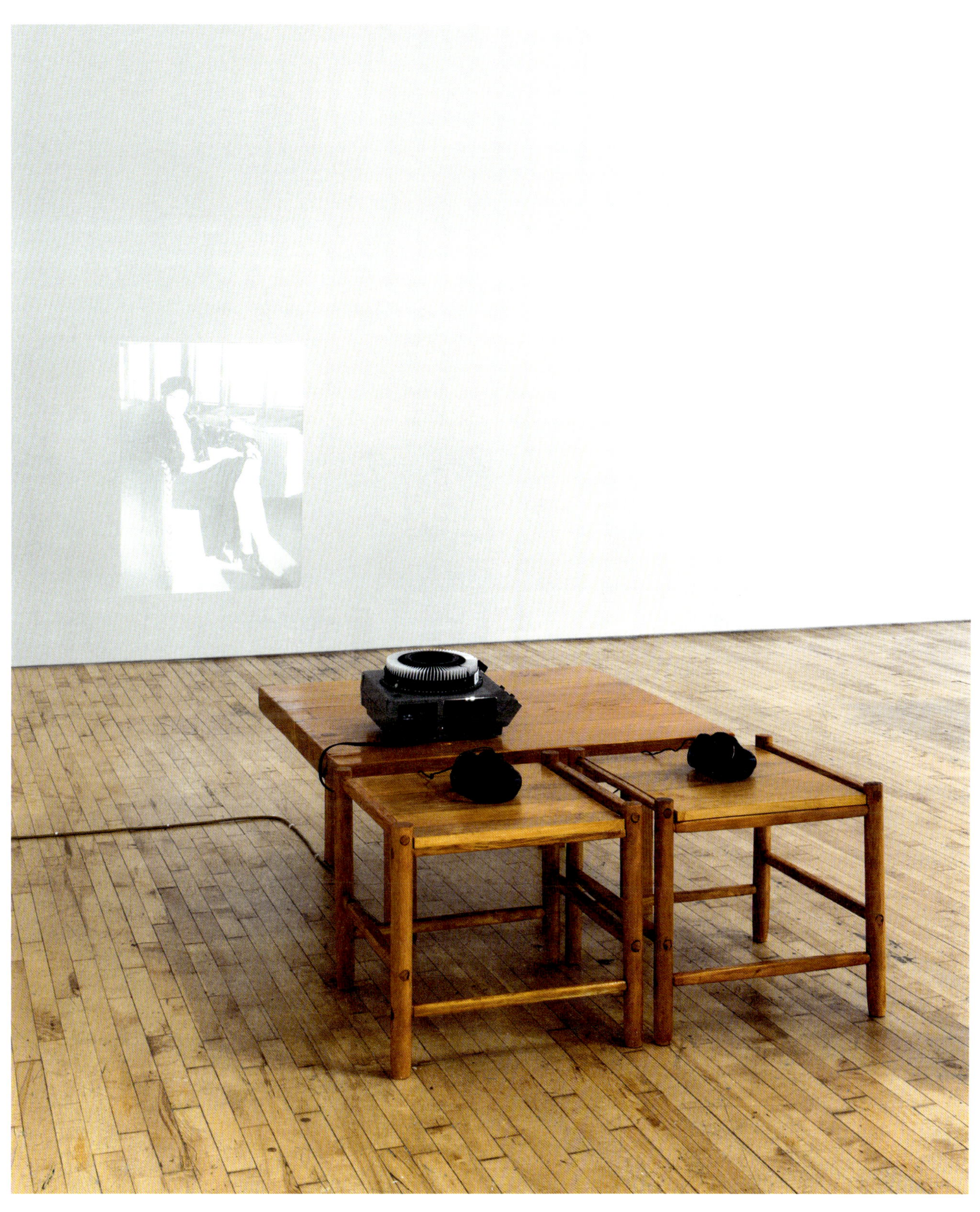

Dearest Federica, 2013

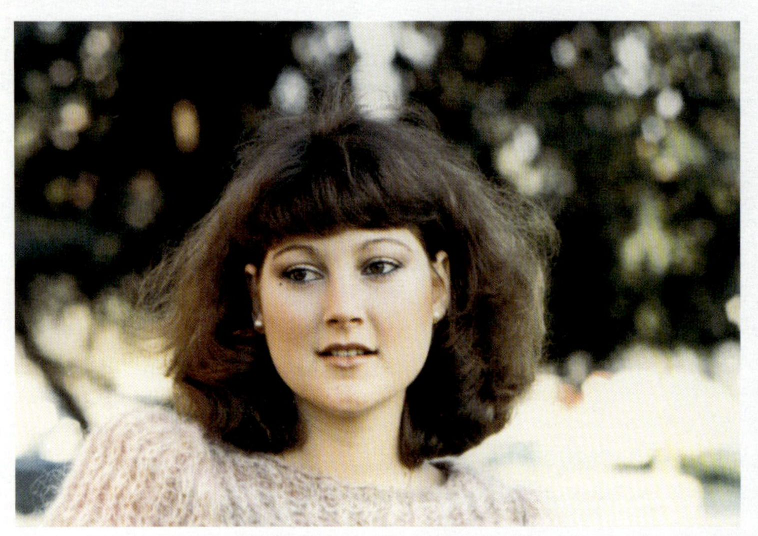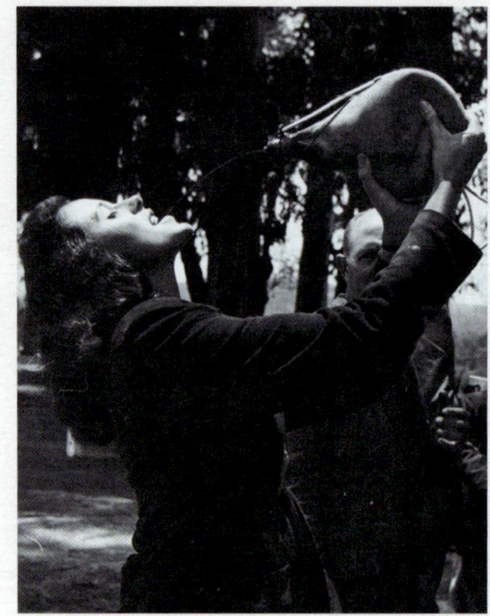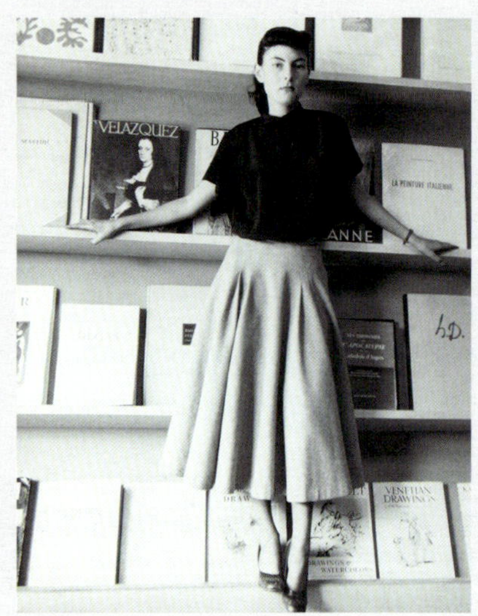

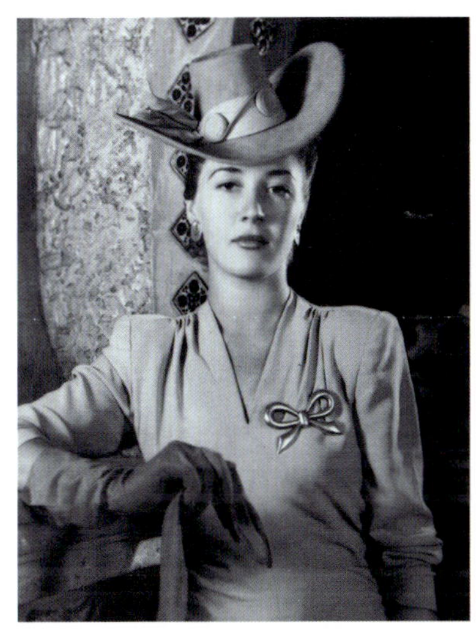 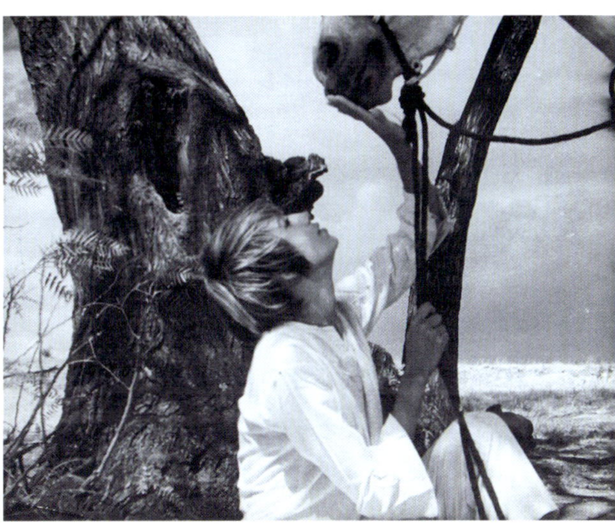 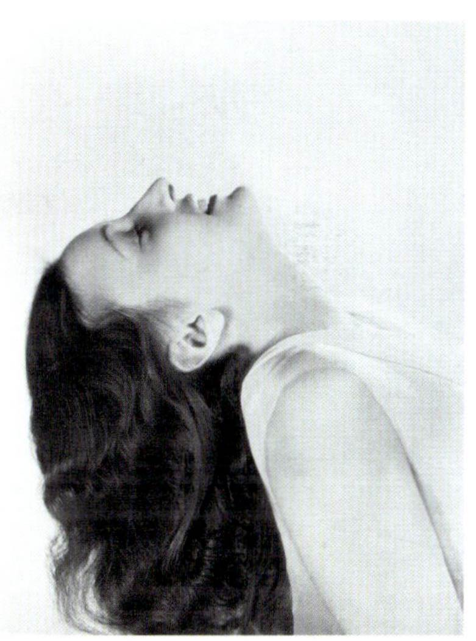

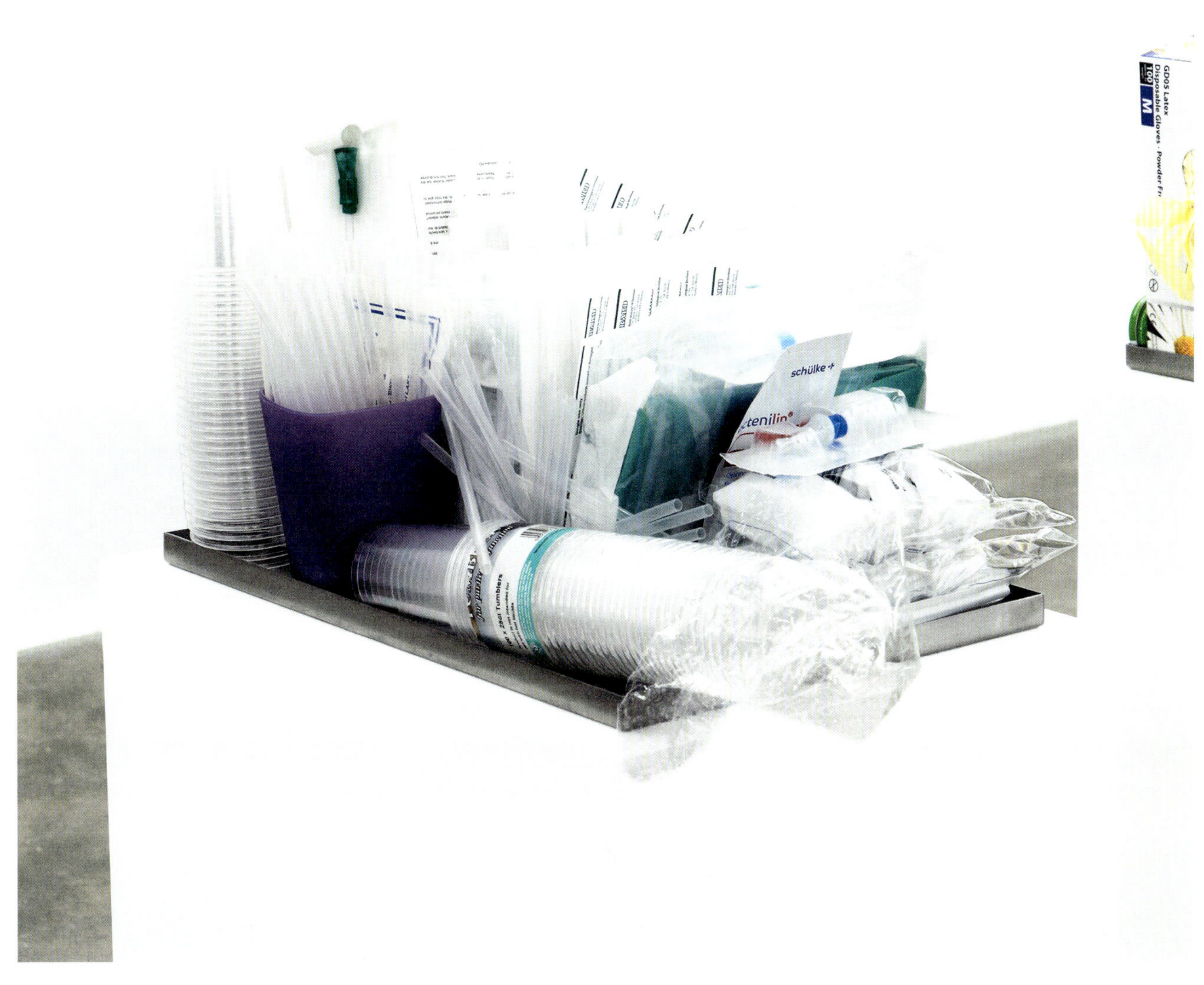

Contact C, 2016

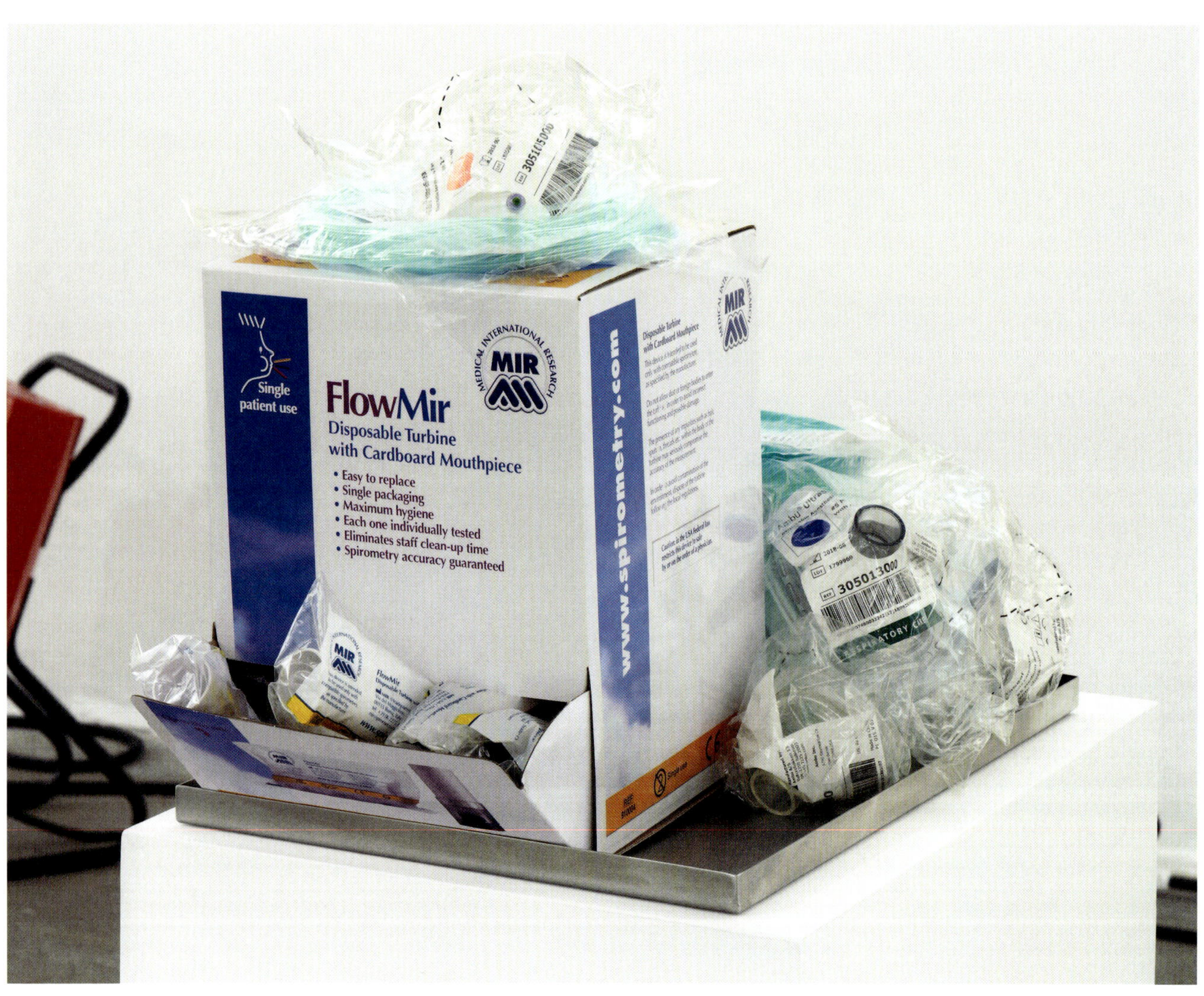

Contact S, 2016

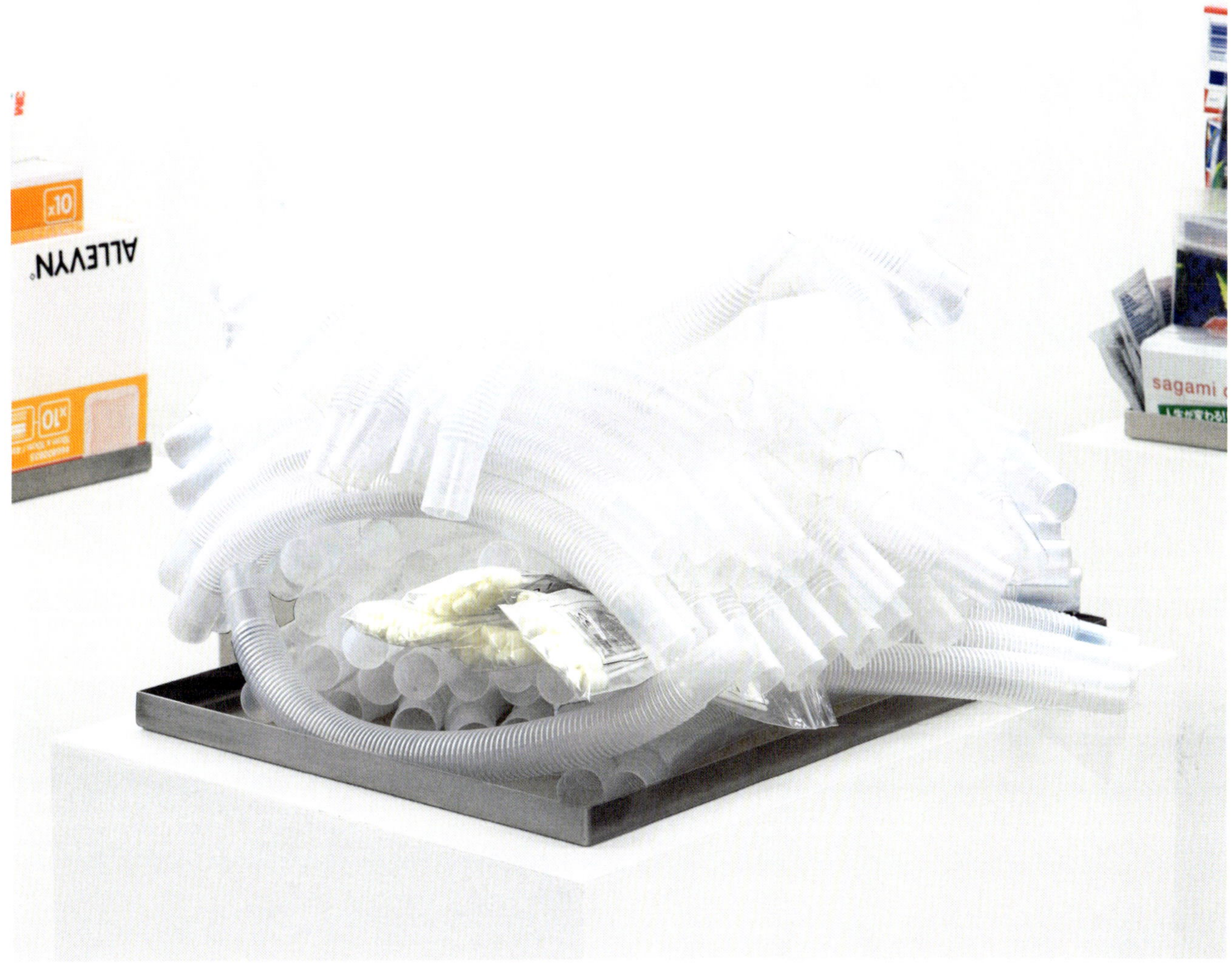

Contact T, 2016

LISA TAN

68

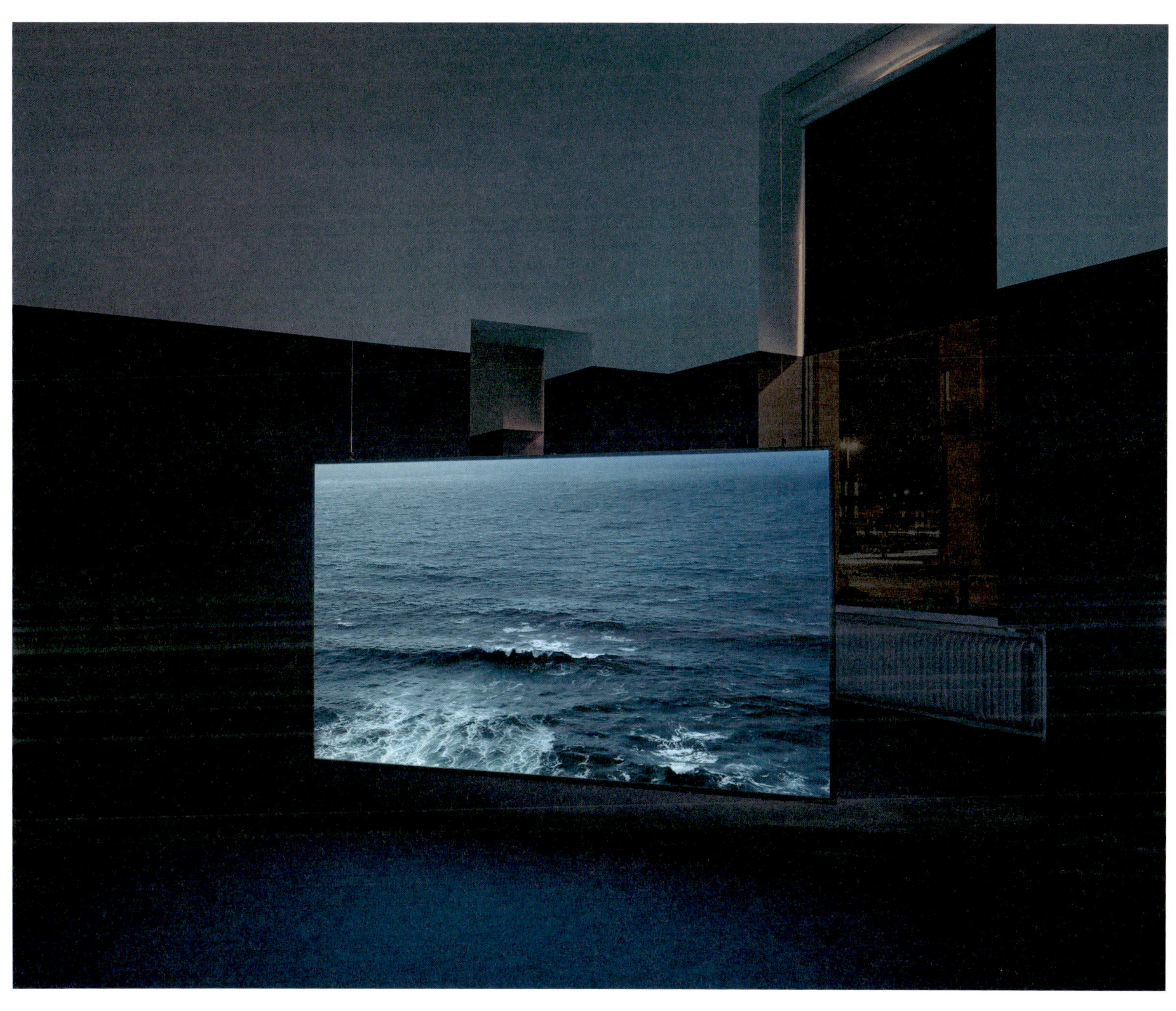

Waves, 2014–15

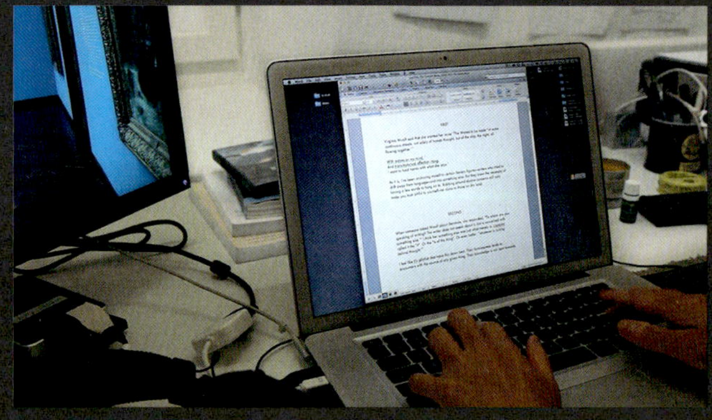

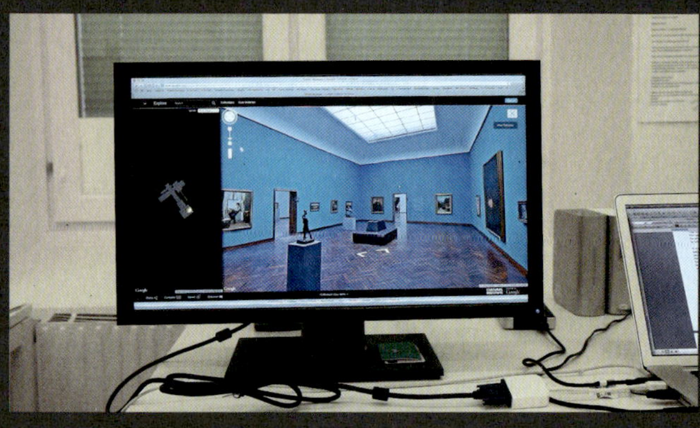
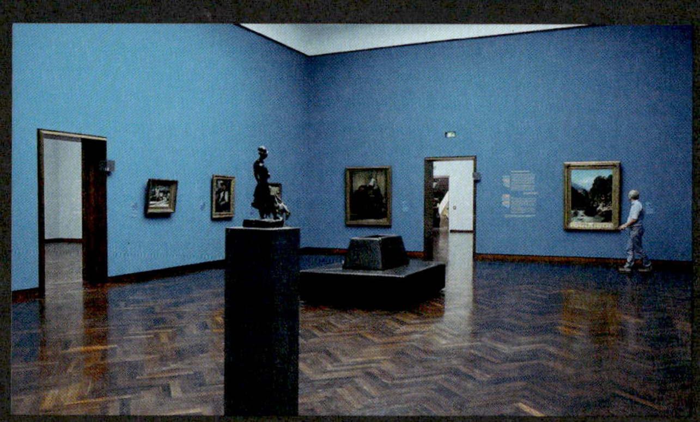

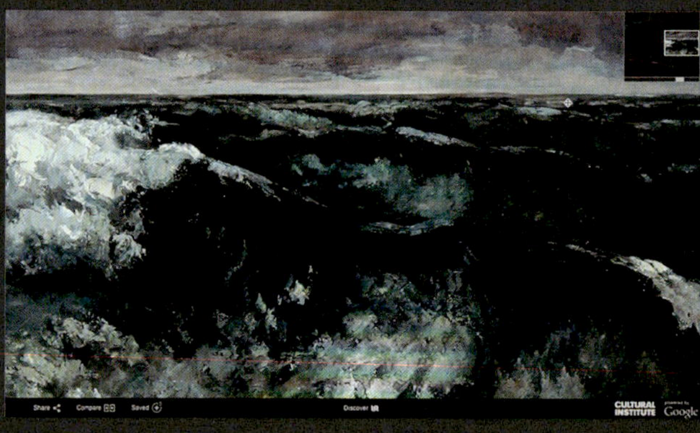
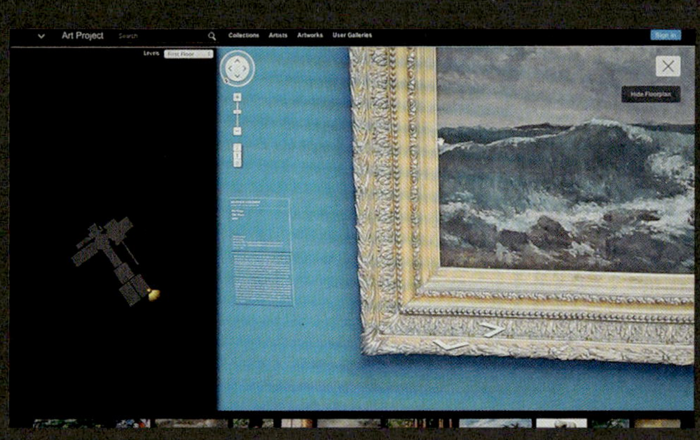
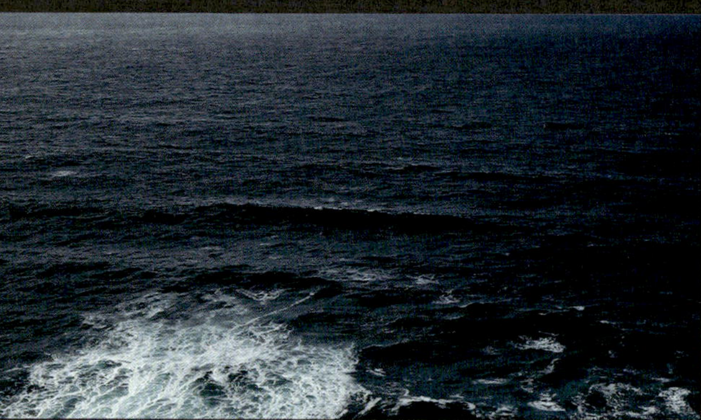

LISA TAN

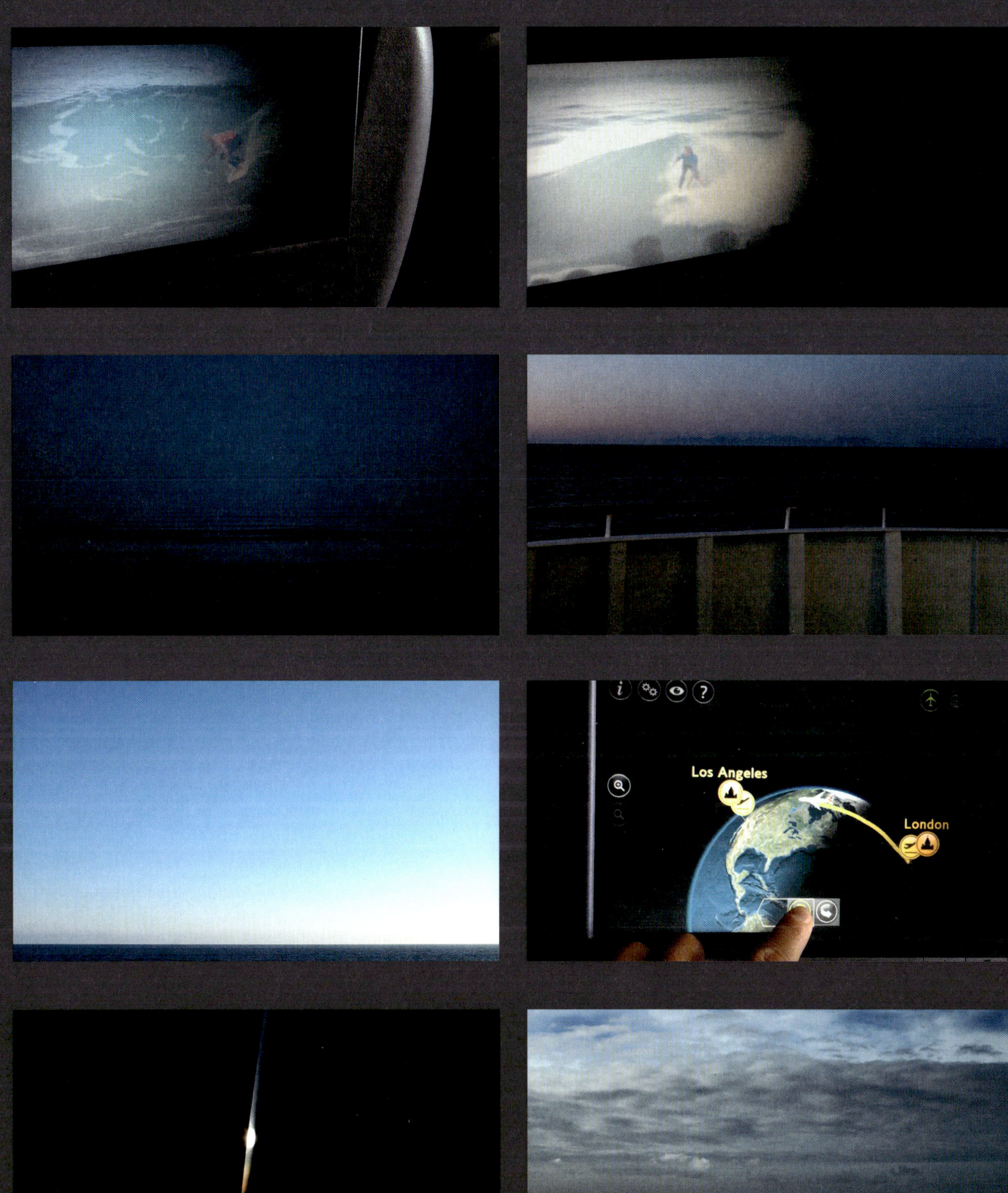

ERIKA VOGT

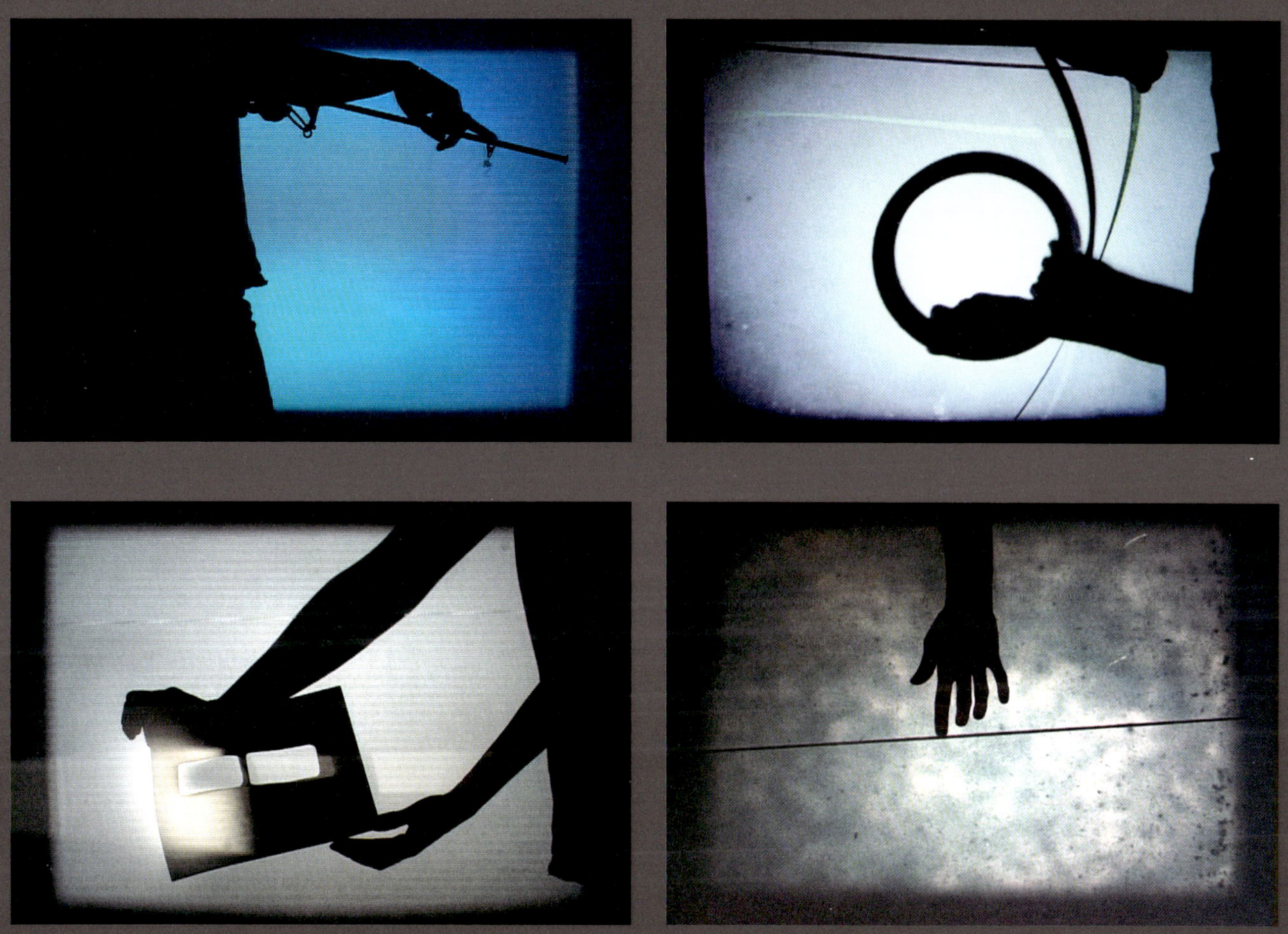

Secret Traveler Navigator, 2010

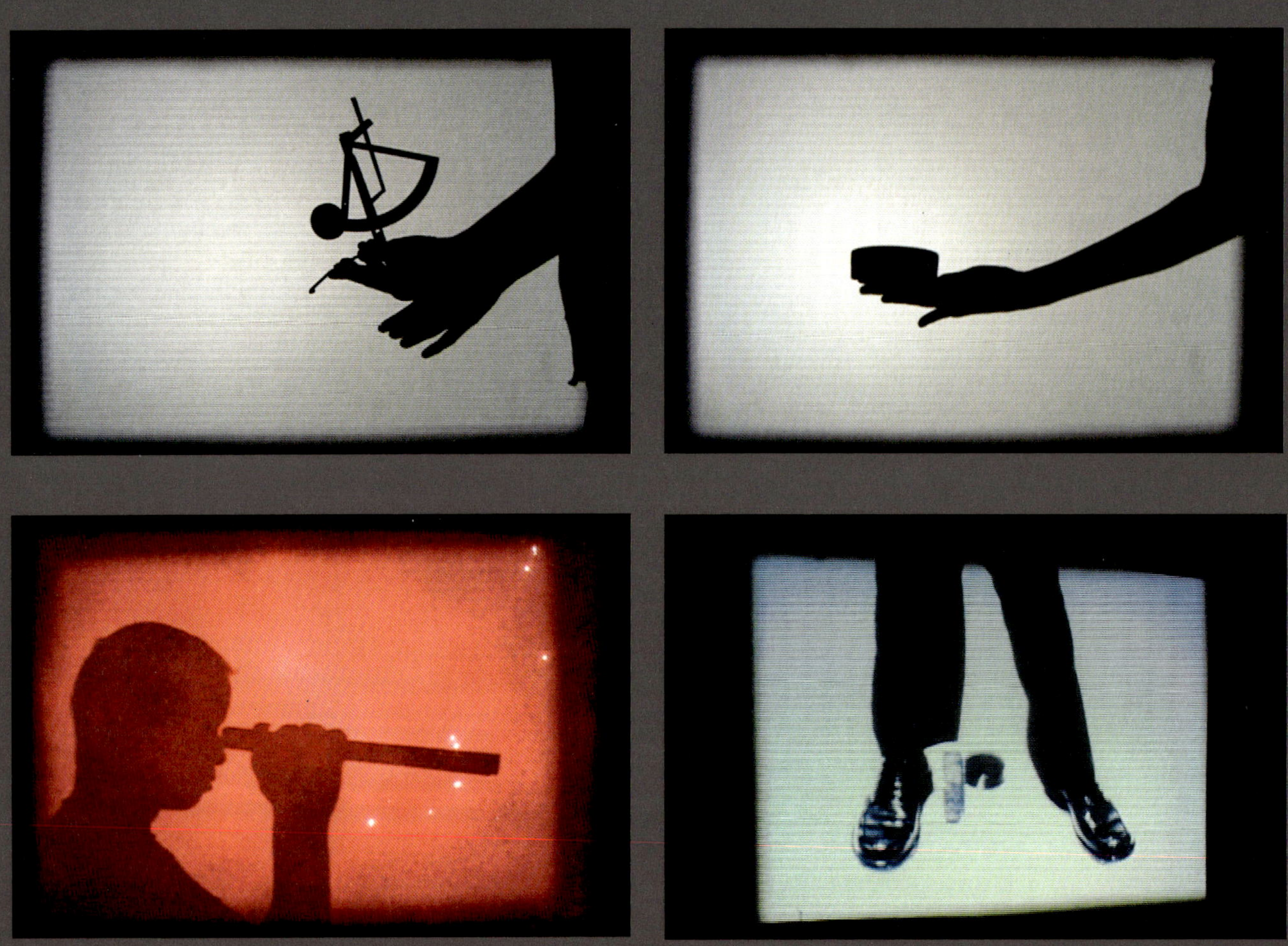

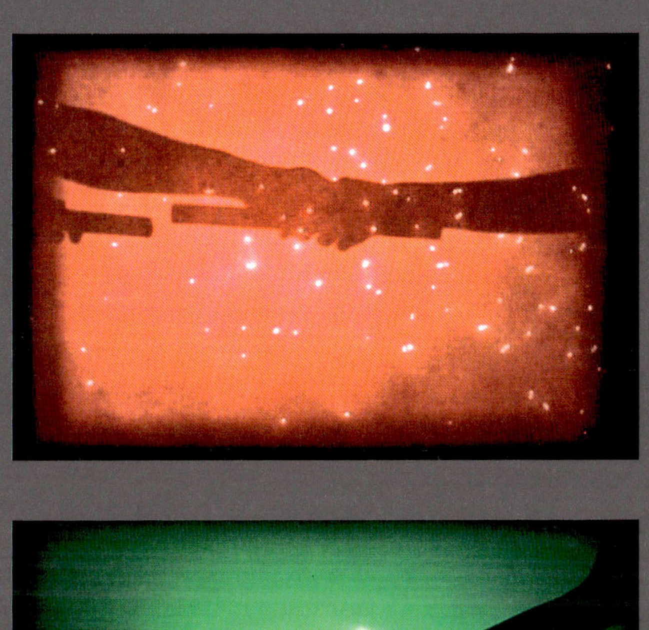
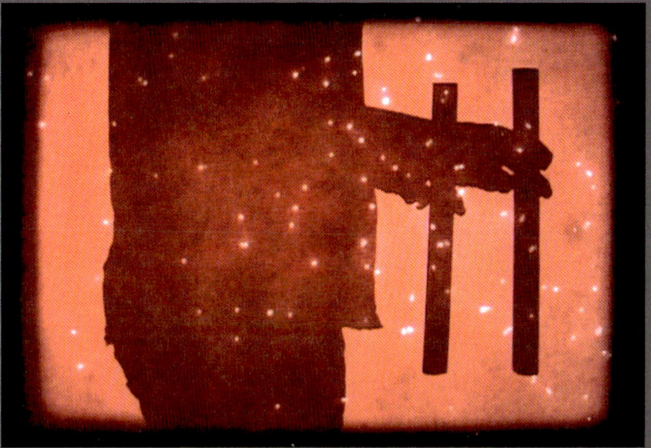
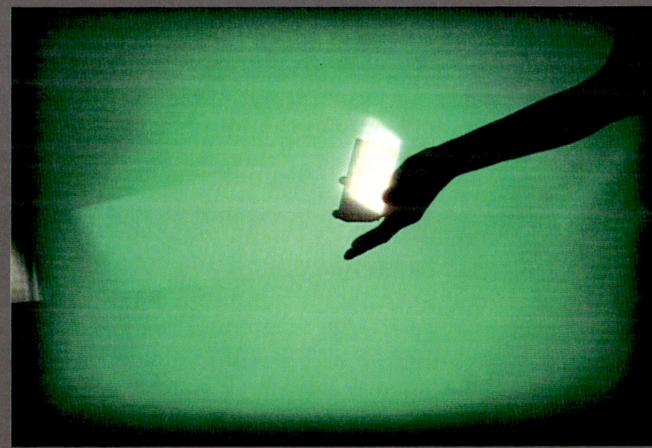
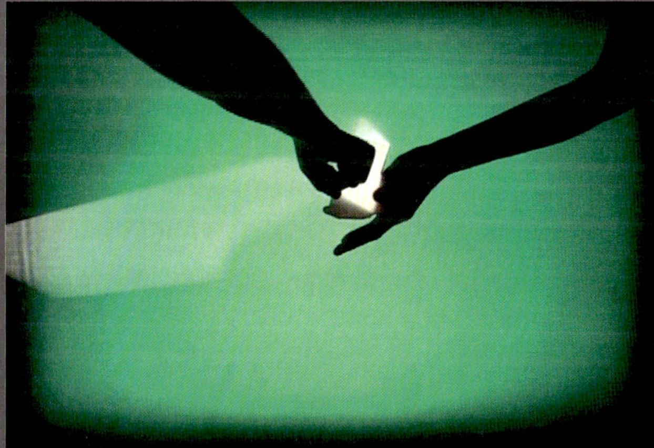

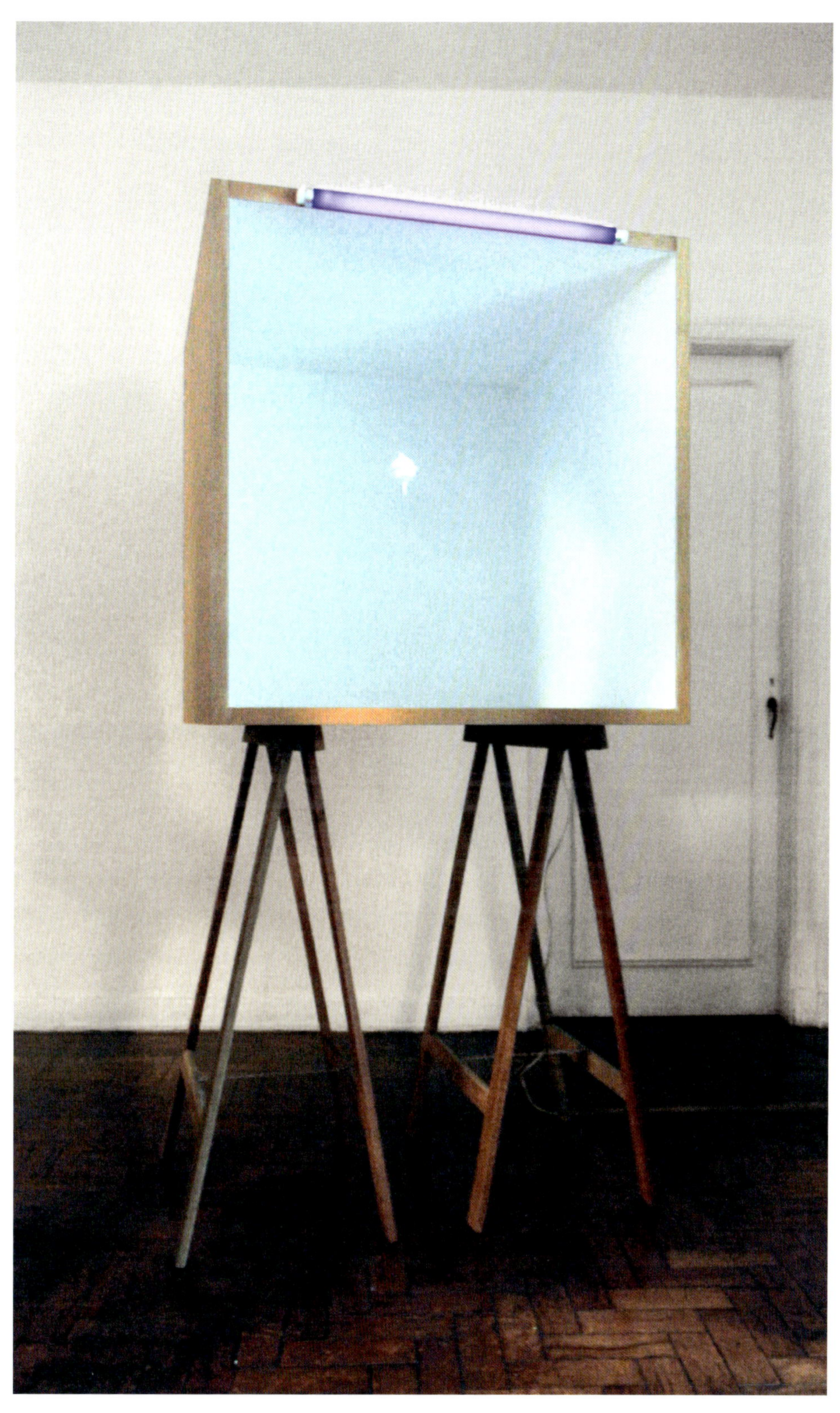

Vertex (Metabolic), 2015

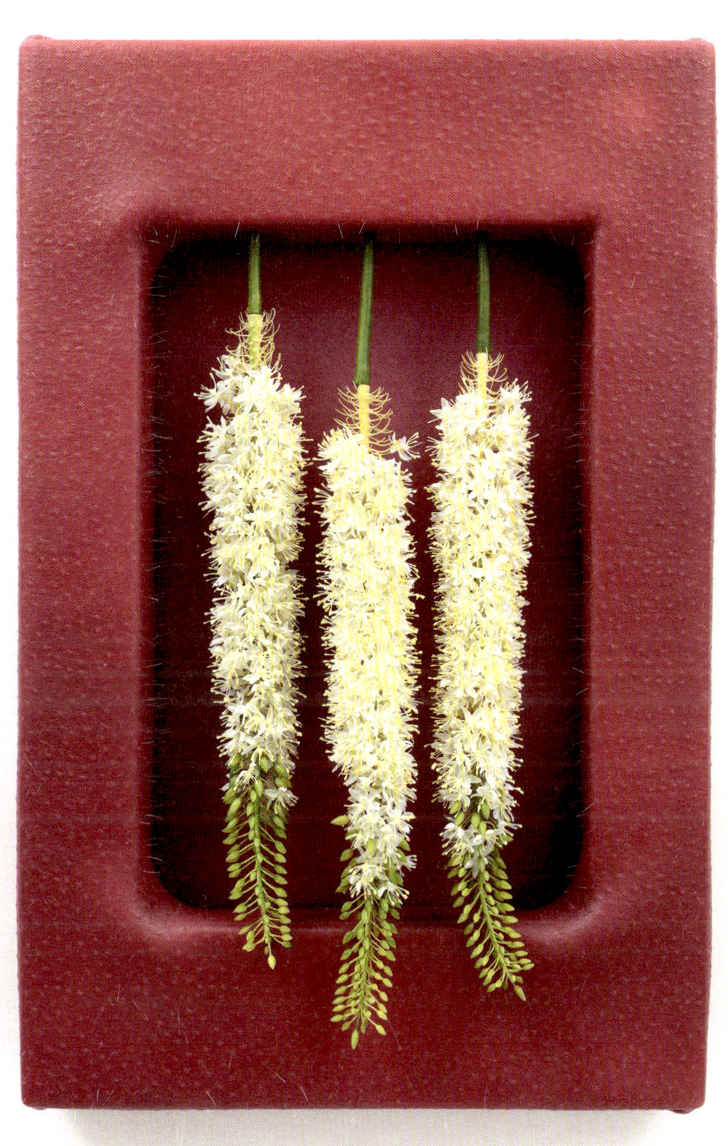

After Democracy, 2016

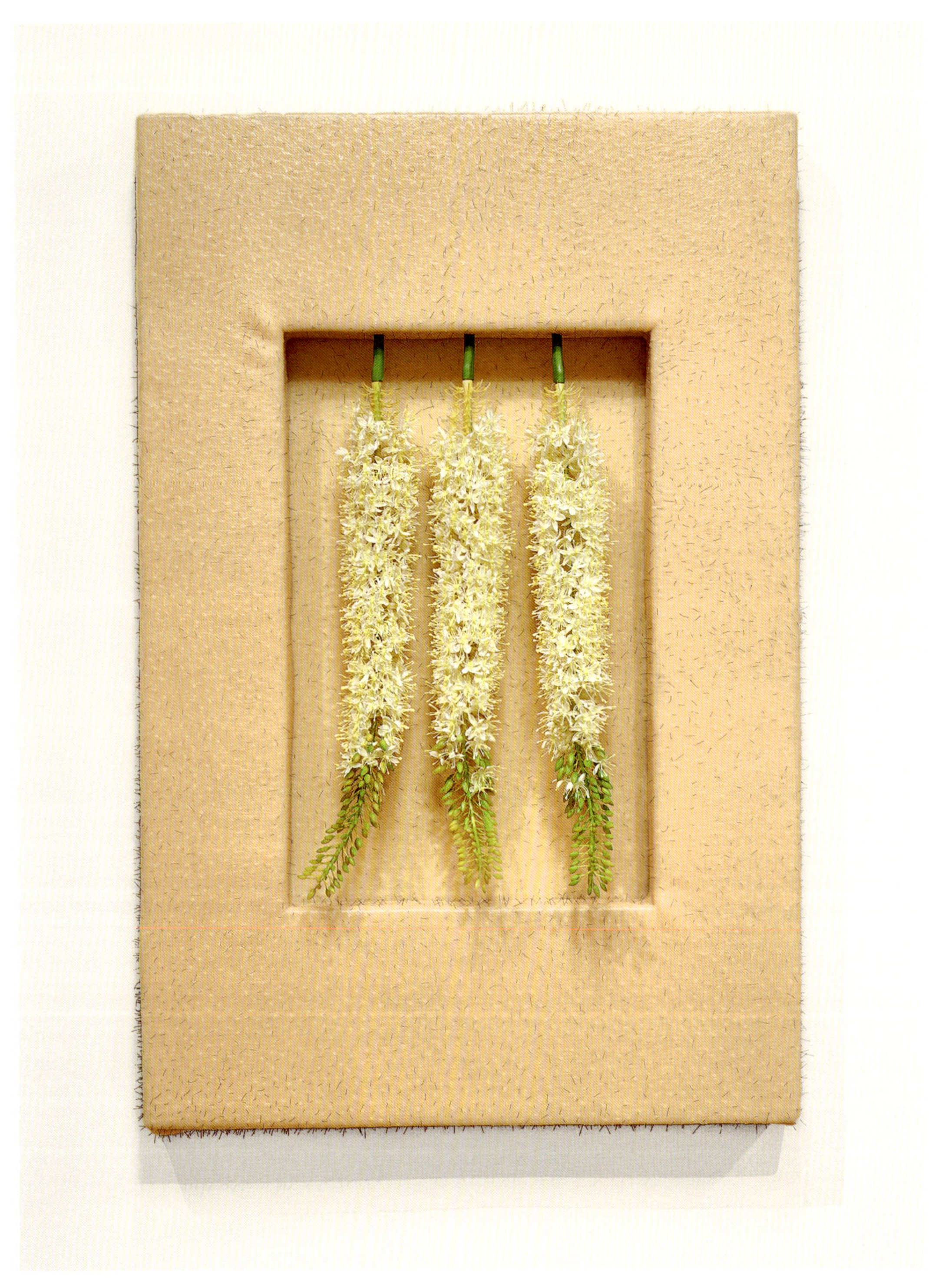

Childless Comfort, 2016

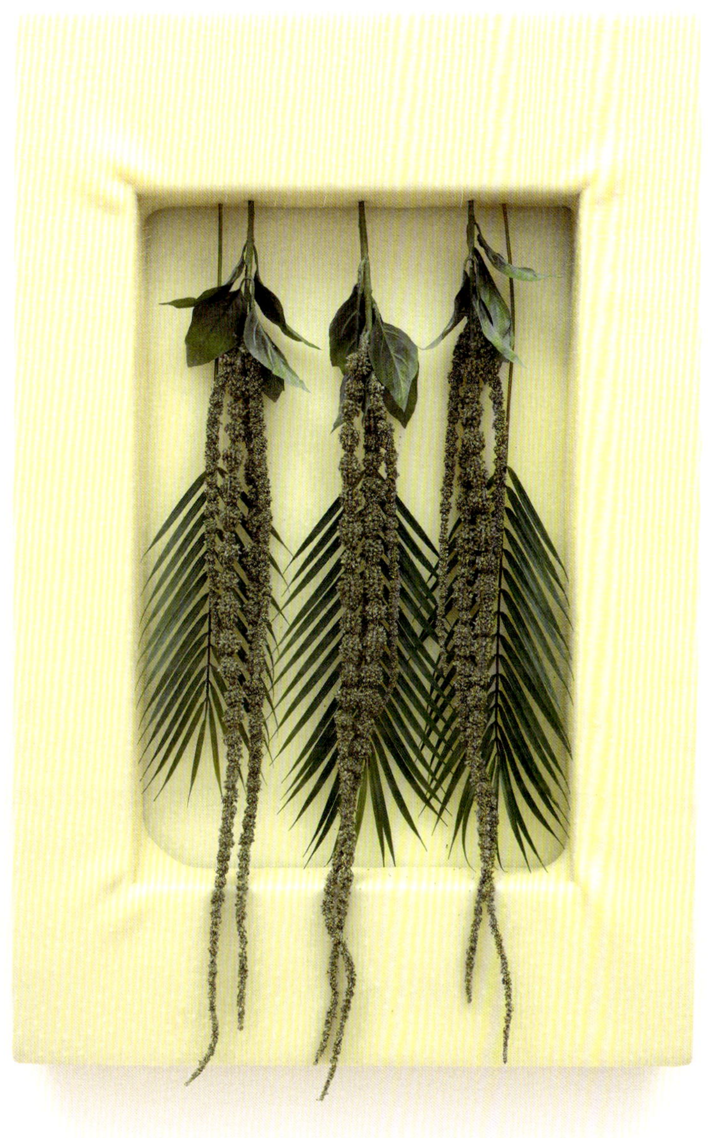

Our Brand Is Crisis, 2016

An Index of Intimacy

EMILY WATLINGTON

Absence

If intimacy is a kind of unity, then the absence of the Other leaves a mark, a breaking point that renders its absence a presence. The mark stands as a witness to a shared experience, signifying the fleeting ephemerality of love and life. It is through such marks that what has passed endures.

"Isn't desire always the same, whether the object is present or absent? Isn't the object always absent?"[1]

The pain of absence must be endured, manipulated, forgotten.

"Absence can exist only as a consequence of the other: it is the other who leaves, it is I who remain."[2]

Closeness

Closeness describes a relational proximity; an "intimate space" is a small one that asks occupants to be close together. What is close is near and familiar.

Because affect is often so personal, we typically disclose it to people who feel close. Relational closeness develops as we self-disclose and surrender the walls that protect our vulnerability through reciprocal sharing of that which is personal— affect, stories, secrets—inviting the Other closer to our depths.

When we want to be close to someone (and want that person to be close in return), we want to be known and cared for (and to know and care for another).

Desire

Will, appetite, libido . . . desire's ruthlessness consumes thought and perturbs identity. Desire is projected onto an object. In turn, the stable object gains the capacity to destabilize its desirer. And the object is never totally objective. Rather, the desirer projects hopes onto it, reimagining specific objects to fit idealized desires. Desire's object, then, is not simply the thing itself but what the desirer hopes it to be; our attachment to desired objects is predicated on possibility.

We hope for desire's fulfillment, but fulfillment is always fleeting, more desire always imminent.

The desirer is creative and optimistic. But desire is also socially regulated, even institutionalized. The individual is encouraged to express and repress desires according to conventions, or what Lauren Berlant calls "hegemonic fantasies," which often take the form of heterosexual monogamy.[3] We are encouraged to hide or shape fantasies to avoid appearing too eager, to avoid being shamed for desiring what others deem undesirable.

"It is my desire I desire, and the loved being is no more than a tool," says Barthes. Or perhaps, as Julia Kristeva claims, the object of desire is a metaphor for the subject: the desirer is a narcissist with an object.[4]

Empathy

To empathize is to mirror the emotion of the Other, to share an affective state. It involves feeling into the object through identification—through seeing oneself in the Other, and through the assimilation of the Other's feelings. Empathy merges the subject and object, prompting the dissolution of individual identity.[5]

And yet, the subject and object always maintain autonomy. I can identify with the Other's misery though it still occurs without me. Sensations felt through the Other arise in my body, shaping my sense of self.

Empathy is shared emotion that converges over relatable experience; it's what compels people to weep during movies and to assist strangers in need. Empathy reveals our limited autonomy, our entanglements, and our capacity to affect one another.[6]

Jealousy

Jealousy draws upon our fear of missing out, our competitive nature, and our tendency to imagine the worst. It can range from a nagging doubt to paranoia, grief, and rage. It is often a projection of insecurity, fear of rejection, fear of abandonment, or feelings of inadequacy. Vanity makes the pangs of jealousy particularly sharp.[7]

"In this condition rage is easily roused; you no longer remember that in love *possession is nothing, enjoyment is everything*. You experience the very worst possible torment, namely, extreme misery still further poisoned by a small remnant of hope."[8]

The anger that often follows jealousy is frequently followed in turn by guilt, shame, or denial. Anger can make us feel empowered in the face of insecurity, but it does not actually make us stronger or safer.[9]

The Other's jealousy can inspire feelings of irritation or hatred, of flattery, of possession, or of disappointment in the Other's lack of trust. Our capacity to evoke jealousy might feel empowering; the Other's jealousy might serve as proof of love.[10]

Loss

"It is possible that one day I will no longer love you, and this possibility cannot be taken away from love— it belongs to it. It is against this possibility, but also with it, that the promise is made."[11]

The possibility, and the fear, of loss, of mourning, exists at love's inception. If love maintains a futurity predicated on individuals' shared wish to flourish together, the possibility of failing to do that—the possibility of loss— always looms. Sometimes, the fear of loss is worse than the loss itself. Sometimes, "I weep for the loss of love, not for him or her."[12]

In French, an orgasm is at times called *une petite mort,* which translates literally to "a little death"—the momentary loss or suspension of self when completely entangled with the Other. This sort of self-loss can be frightening but also beautiful. Loss of the Other brings about a different kind of loss of self: "I have projected myself into the other with such power that when I am without the other I cannot recover myself, regain myself: I am lost, forever."[13]

Love

"Love is double, conflictual, or ambivalent: necessary and impossible, sweet and bitter, free and chained, spiritual and sensual, enlivening and mortal, lucid and blind, altruistic and egotistic."[14]

The basis of joy in love is that we feel our existence valued, justified.[15]

And so, we tell our loved ones over and over again (and want to hear them say) that we love them (that they love us). For the possibility that the promise of love is fleeting is part of what makes it so passionate. The affective attachments formed with beloved objects fluctuate: "intimacy relies heavily on the shifting registers of unspoken ambivalence."[16] Committed love endures despite this—it sustains desire's optimism, the shared wish of individuals to flourish together. It is an intimate experience of the sublime; it is "to derive pleasure from seeing, touching, and feeling through all one's senses and as closely as possible, a lovable person who loves us."[17]

Love is not merely the total possession of the Other; if that were so, it would be easily attained. Instead, it is the unrealizable ideal of total unity with the Other—the appropriation of the Other's freedom that still sustains its freeness.[18]

Reciprocity

"[Intimacy] consists as much in taking as in giving, as much in requiring as in renouncing."[19]

To love is to want to be loved; loving is the project of making oneself lovable. And yet, love requires self-sacrifice; it is a give and take of support, rendering the sacrifice mutual. Mutual indebtedness creates the condition for interdependency within intimate entanglements. Indebtedness here should not be thought of as a debt that follows a transaction but rather a debt that is the condition of the possibility of ongoing mutual support.[20]

Reciprocity can be negative—we sometimes reciprocate the Other's unfavorable behavior in an effort to attain fairness, to settle the debt. Negative or positive, reciprocity is cyclical; the debt is never settled.

To be loved or desired is to become an object; even mature love is not above objectification.[21] When we call the Other "cute" or "adorable," we remark upon and take delight in the Other's endearing subordinance. Reciprocity can never realize constant equality but rather takes turns being up and down.[22]

Seduction

Seduction is deception, artifice, signs, game, ritual, challenge, and charm.

"It is a power of attraction and distraction, of absorption and fascination."[23]

Seduction is both carnal and strategic. It is a game: "To be seduced is to challenge the other to be seduced in turn."[24]

Being seduced can be flattering. Yet, simultaneously, it is impersonal— a ritual that turns the seducee into an object.[25] Seduction can frighten, threatening the seducee's will and self-control. Seducers, likewise, aim to turn themselves into objects of desire in order to act as desiring subjects— for to desire is to want to be desired.

Shame

"Shame is an experience of the self by the self."[26] It involves, terrifyingly, an exaggerated awareness of being looked at by others.

We feel shame when we expose something personal and expect acceptance or affirmation but are instead met with indifference or contempt. We are susceptible to shame when confessing love, sharing work, revealing secrets. Shame, then, is linked to our desire for intimacy and identification. It occurs when our openness is not reciprocated. Gradually, we release shyness (the fear of being shamed) in intimate relationships in which, over time, we are repeatedly accepted and affirmed.

Looking into another's eyes, affect becomes contagious. This sharing creates intimacy and vulnerability. But shame prompts a desire to hide, a wish to no longer be vulnerable, a longing both to continue being looked at and also not to be.

"[Adam and Eve] were both naked, and they felt no shame" in Edenic intimacy; they exposed themselves and were met with unconditional acceptance.[27]

Trust

Trust makes exchange possible in the face of uncertainty or unpredictability. It requires an extrarational dimension that is necessarily optimistic. Trust is gradable—we can trust someone or something to a degree.

And to a degree in daily life we must trust strangers—strangers who share public spaces with us, prepare our food, operate the heavy machinery that pours through our cities and highways. Systems of interdependency require trust; we must rely on one another all the time, and without trust, we would not be able to do much of anything at all. Trust allows us to feel secure with fellow humans.

We tend to believe a stranger's words to be true until given a reason to believe otherwise. Over time, trust ideally increases with familiarity, unless familiarity proves the Other untrustworthy.[28]

Vulnerability

"This is what one gives above all in love: the condition of possibility for a laying waste."[29]

To open oneself to intimacy is to open oneself to rejection or loss. To allow the Other to come closer is to permit the breaking of boundaries. Vulnerability "connote[s] weakness, softness, permeability, a sense of being affected, imprinted upon, or entered and shattered."[30]

Vulnerability is at once the fear of the possibility of an impending affect, and an affect itself; Ulrika Dahl calls it "the affective state of openness."[31]

We are often inclined to focus attention on the negative rather than the positive; much more theoretical writing considers negative rather than positive affects. And so we fear love because it renders us vulnerable. Asks Kristeva, "Shaky voice, dry throat, starry eyes, flushed or clammy skin, throbbing heart ... Would the symptoms of love be the symptoms of fear?"[32]

Notes

[1] Roland Barthes, *A Lover's Discourse: Fragments* (New York: Hill and Wang, 1978), 15.

[2] Ibid., 13.

[3] Berlant, *Intimacy* (Chicago: University of Chicago Press, 2000), 6.

[4] Kristeva, *Tales of Love* (New York: Columbia University Press, 1987), 33. Kristeva uses *love* in lieu of *desire* in her text, but my writing builds upon Lauren Berlant's distinction of love and desire (see Berlant, *Desire/Love* [New York: Dead Letter Office, 2012], 6–7).

[5] Juliet Koss, "On the Limits of Empathy," *Art Bulletin* 88, no. 1 (2006): 139–57.

[6] Lauren Berlant in Lydialyle Gibson, "Mirrored Emotion," *University of Chicago Magazine* 98 (April 2006).

[7] Stendhal, *On Love*, trans. H. B. V. (New York: Liveright Publishing, 1947), 119.

[8] Ibid., 118.

[9] Dossie Easton and Janet W. Hardy, "Roadmaps through Jealousy," in *The Ethical Slut: A Practical Guide to Polyamory, Open Relationships, and Other Adventures* (New York: Celestial Arts, 1997), 108–30.

[10] Stendhal, *On Love*, 124.

[11] Jean-Luc Nancy, "Shattered Love," in *The Inoperative Community*, trans. Peter Connor (Minneapolis: University of Minnesota Press, 1991), 100.

[12] Barthes, *A Lover's Discourse*, 31.

[13] Ibid., 49.

[14] Nancy, "Shattered Love," 87.

[15] Jean-Paul Sartre, "First Attitude Toward Others: Love, Language, Masochism," in *Being and Nothingness: An Essay on Phenomenological Ontology*, trans. Hazel Estella Barnes (London: Routledge, 2003), 393.

[16] Berlant, *Intimacy*, 6.

[17] Nancy, "Shattered Love," 97, and Stendhal, *On Love*, 5.

[18] Sartre, "First Attitude Toward Others," 389.

[19] Nancy, "Shattered Love," 101.

[20] Karen Barad, "On Touching—The Inhuman That Therefore I Am," *differences* 23 (2012): 206–23.

[21] Sartre, "First Attitude Toward Others," 397.

[22] William Ian Miller, *The Anatomy of Disgust* (Cambridge, MA: Harvard University Press, 1997), 32.

[23] Jean Baudrillard, *Seduction* (New York: St. Martin's Press, 1990), 81.

[24] Ibid., 22.

[25] Sartre, "First Attitude Toward Others," 394.

[26] Silvan Tomkins, *Shame and Its Sisters: A Silvan Tomkins Reader*, ed. Eve Kosofsky Sedgwick and Adam Frank (Durham, NC: Duke University Press, 1995), 136.

[27] Genesis 2:25 (New International Version).

[28] Lars Svendsen, *A Philosophy of Fear* (London: Reaktion Books, 2008), 98.

[29] Eugenie Brinkema, "On No Longer Being Loved: Eleven Formal Problems Related to Method," *Cine-files*, no. 10 (Spring 2016).

[30] Ulrika Dahl, "Femmebodiment: Notes on Queer Shapes of Vulnerability," *Feminist Theory* 17 (2016): 7.

[31] Ibid., 9.

[32] Kristeva, *Tales of Love*, 6.

Andrea Büttner (b. 1972, Germany; lives and works in London and Frankfurt am Main, Germany)—Büttner's solo exhibitions include *Beggars and iPhones* (2016) at Kunsthalle Wien; *Andrea Büttner* (2015) at the Walker Art Center, Minneapolis; and *The Poverty of Riches* (2011) at Whitechapel Gallery, London. Her work has been included in group exhibitions such as *Documenta 13* (2012); *Individual Stories: Sammeln als Porträt und Methodologie* (2015) at Kunsthalle Wien, Austria; and *A Prosu(u)mer Reader* (2015) at Contemporary Art Museum Estonia, Tallinn.

Sophie Calle (b. 1943, France; lives and works in Malakoff, France)—Calle's solo exhibitions include *Last Seen* (2013) at Isabella Stewart Gardner Museum, Boston; *Prenez soin de vous* (2007) in the French Pavilion at the 52nd Venice Biennale; and *M'as-tu vue* (2003) at the Centre Georges Pompidou, Paris. Her work has been included in group exhibitions such as *The Memory of Time* (2015) at the National Gallery of Art in Washington, D.C.; *WITNESS* (2016) at the Museum of Contemporary Art, Chicago; and *Manifesta 11* (2016).

Alejandro Cesarco (b. 1975, Uruguay; lives and works in New York)—Cesarco's solo exhibitions include *A Portrait, a Story, and an Ending* (2013) at Kunsthalle Zürich; *Baloise Kunst Preis 2012* (2012) at Museum Moderner Kunst Stiftung Ludwig, Vienna; and *A Common Ground* (2011) in the Uruguay Pavilion at the 54th Venice Biennale. His work has been included in group exhibitions such as *Under the Same Sun: Art from Latin America Today* (2014) at the Solomon R. Guggenheim Museum, New York; *New Ways of Doing Nothing* (2014) at Kunsthalle Wien, Austria; and the 30th Bienal Internacional de São Paulo (2012).

Jason Dodge (b. 1969, United States; lives and works in Berlin)—Dodge is an artist, as well as publisher and editor of the poetry press fivehundred places.

Felix Gonzalez-Torres (1957–1996, United States, b. Cuba)—Gonzalez-Torres's solo exhibitions include *Felix Gonzalez-Torres: Specific Objects Without Specific Form* (2010–11) at WIELS, Brussels; *Felix Gonzalez-Torres: America* (2007) in the U.S. Pavilion at the 52nd Venice Biennale; and *Felix Gonzalez-Torres: Traveling* (1994) at the Hirshhorn Museum and Sculpture Garden, Washington, D.C.; the Museum of Contemporary Art, Los Angeles; and the Renaissance Society, Chicago. His work has been included in group exhibitions such as *America Is Hard to See* (2015) at the Whitney Museum of American Art, New York; *Getting Emotional* (2005) at the Institute of Contemporary Art, Boston; and *A Day Without Art* (1996) at the Museum of Contemporary Art, Los Angeles.

Antonia Hirsch (b. 1968, Germany; lives and works in Berlin)—Hirsch's solo exhibitions include *Negative Space* (2014–15) at Gallery TPW, Toronto, and Simon Fraser University Galleries, Vancouver, and *Komma* (2012) at Tramway, Glasgow. Her work has been included in group exhibitions such as *Art in the Age of . . . Planetary Computation* (2015) at Witte de With Center for Contemporary Art, Rotterdam; *Punctum* (2014) at Salzburger Kunstverein, Austria; and *It Is What It Is* (2010) at the National Gallery of Canada, Ottawa.

Jill Magid (b. 1973, United States; lives and works in New York)—Magid's solo exhibitions include *The Proposal* (2016) at Kunsthalle Sankt Gallen, Switzerland, and the San Francisco Art Institute; *A Reasonable Man in a Box* (2010) at the Whitney Museum of American Art, New York; and *Authority to Remove* (2009) at Tate Modern, London. Her work has been included in group exhibitions such as *Electronic Superhighway* (2016) at Whitechapel Gallery, London; *Manifesta 11* (2016); and *After Belonging* (2016) at the Cincinnati Art Museum, Ohio.

Park McArthur (b. 1984, United States; lives and works in New York)—McArthur's solo exhibitions include *Poly* (2016) at Chisenhale Gallery, London; *Passive Vibration Isolation* (2014) at Lars Friedrich, Berlin; and *During the month of August ESSEX STREET will be closed.* (2013) at ESSEX STREET, New York. Her work has been included in group exhibitions such as the 32nd Bienal Internacional de São Paulo (2016); *Greater New York* (2015) at MoMA PS1, New York; and *Senses of Care: Mediated Ability and Interdependence* (2014) at G@C2, University of Southern California, San Diego.

Lisa Tan (b. 1973, United States; lives and works in Stockholm)—Tan's solo exhibitions include *Notes From Underground* (2017) at Kunsthall Trondheim, Norway; *For Every Word Has Its Own Shadow* (2015) at Galleri Riis, Stockholm; and *Sunsets* (2014) at Museum of Contemporary Art, Santa Barbara. Her work has been included in group exhibitions such as *ever elusive: thirty years of transmediale* at Haus der Kulturen der Welt, Berlin (2017); the 11th Shanghai Biennale (2016); and *Surround Audience*, the New Museum Triennial (2015), New York.

Erika Vogt (b. 1973, United States; lives and works in Los Angeles)—Vogt's solo exhibitions include *Eros Island: Knives Please Rise* (2016) at Overduin & Co., Los Angeles; *SPEECH MESH—Drawn OFF* (2015) at the Hepworth Wakefield, England; and *Stranger Debris Roll Roll Roll* (2013) at the New Museum, New York. Her work has been included in group exhibitions such as *Reconstructions: Recent Photographs and Video from the Met Collection* (2015) at the Metropolitan Museum, New York, and *Made in LA* (2012) at the Hammer Museum, Los Angeles. Performa commissioned her theatrical piece *Artist Theater Program: Lava plus Knives* in 2015.

Susanne M. Winterling (b. 1970, Germany; lives and works in Berlin and Oslo)—Winterling's solo exhibitions include *The Front Room* (2009) at Contemporary Art Museum, St. Louis; *The Inscribable Surface* (2012) at Salzburger Kunstverein, Austria; and *Complicity* (2014) at Kunstverein Amsterdam. Her work has been included in group exhibitions such as *Liebe Deine Maschine* (2015) at Kunstverein Hildesheim, Germany; *A Disagreeable Object* (2012) at SculptureCenter, New York; and the Fifth Berlin Biennale (2008).

Anicka Yi (b. 1971, South Korea; lives and works in New York)—Yi's solo exhibitions include *6,070,430K of Digital Spit* (2015) at the MIT List Visual Arts Center and Kunsthalle Basel; *Jungle Stripe* (2016) at Fridericianum, Kassel, Germany; and *You Can Call Me F* (2016) at the Kitchen, New York. Her work has been included in group exhibitions such as the 11th Gwangju Biennale, South Korea (2016); the 12th Biennale de Lyon (2013); and *Das Ding!* (2013) at Swiss Institute / Contemporary Art, New York.

Andrea Büttner

Brown Wall Painting, 2006
Interior emulsion paint
Dimensions vary with installation
Courtesy the artist; Hollybush Gardens, London;
and David Kordansky Gallery, Los Angeles

Little Works, 2007
Single-channel HD video with sound, 10:42 min.
Courtesy the artist and Hollybush Gardens, London

Tent (psychedelic), 2012
Woodcut print on paper
61¼ x 55⅛ in. (155.6 x 140 cm)
Courtesy the artist and David Kordansky Gallery,
Los Angeles

Curtain, 2013
Woodcut print on paper, ed. 5/10, plus 2 a.p.
55⅛ x 78 in. (140 x 198.1 cm)
Courtesy the artist and David Kordansky Gallery,
Los Angeles

Sophie Calle

Secrets, 2014
Two safes, engraved plaque, and framed contract,
ed. 5/7, plus 2 a.p.
Each safe: 8 x 10 x 8 in. (20.3 x 25.4 x 20.3 cm),
plaque (in French or English): 2⅞ x 4 x ⅛ in. (7.3 x
10.2 x .3 cm), contract: 14 x 19 x 1 in. (35.6 x 48.3 x
2.5 cm); overall dimensions vary with installation
Collection Alex Hank; courtesy the artist and
Paula Cooper Gallery, New York

Alejandro Cesarco

*Fragile Images That Keep Producing Death
While Attempting to Preserve Life:
Flowers found in crime scenes_001–004*, 2011
Archival inkjet prints, ed. of 5
Four units, each 28 x 21 in. (71 x 53 cm)
Courtesy the artist and Tanya Leighton
Gallery, Berlin

Jason Dodge

Anyone

Felix Gonzalez-Torres

"Untitled" (Loverboy), 1989
Blue fabric and hanging device
Dimensions vary with installation
Private collection, New York

Antonia Hirsch

Object T, 2015
Single-channel HD video installation with
heated bench, 12:06 min.
Dimensions vary with installation
Courtesy the artist and Republic Gallery,
Vancouver

Black Echo, 2017
Glass, steel, and Plexiglas
Object: 7⅞ x 2¹⁵⁄₁₆ x 5½ in. (7 x 14 x 20 cm),
stand: 37¹⁵⁄₁₆ x 15½ x 31⅛ in. (39 x 79 x 96 cm),
Plexiglas: 13 x 21⁵⁄₁₆ x 36³⁄₁₆ in. (54 x 92 x 33 cm)
Courtesy the artist and Republic Gallery,
Vancouver

Jill Magid

Dearest Federica, 2013
80 slides, slide projector, and low table
after Luis Barragán
Dimensions vary with installation
Courtesy the artist; Labor, Mexico City;
and Untilthen, Paris

Park McArthur

Contact C, 2016
Plastic cup, disposable cups, drinking straws,
catheter kit, enema kit parts, travel toilets,
cleaning solution, lubricant, latex gloves,
and stainless-steel tray
Stainless-steel tray: ¾ x 16¾ x 12 in.
(1.9 x 42.6 x 30.5 cm), plinth: 33 x 19 x 14 in.
(83.8 x 48.3 x 35.6 cm); overall dimensions
vary with installation
Collection Carlomar Rios

Contact S, 2016
Disposable mouthpieces, masks, cannulas,
and stainless-steel tray
Stainless-steel tray: ¾ x 16¾ x 12 in. (1.9 x
42.6 x 30.5 cm), plinth: 33 x 19 x 14 in.
(83.8 x 48.3 x 35.6 cm); overall dimensions
vary with installation
Courtesy the artist and ESSEX STREET, New York

Contact T, 2016
Tubing, swabs, and stainless-steel tray
Stainless-steel tray: ¾ x 16¾ x 12 in.
(1.9 x 42.6 x 30.5 cm), plinth: 33 x 19 x 14 in.
(83.8 x 48.3 x 35.6 cm); overall dimensions
vary with installation
Courtesy the artist and ESSEX STREET, New York

Lisa Tan

Waves, 2014–15
Single-channel HD video with sound, 19:12 min.
Courtesy the artist and Galleri Riis, Oslo

Erika Vogt

Secret Traveler Navigator, 2010
Single-channel digital video installation,
sound, 13:23 min.
Dimensions vary with installation
Courtesy the artist and Overduin & Co.,
Los Angeles

Susanne M. Winterling

Vertex (Metabolic), 2015
Medium-density fiberboard, steel, black-light
bulb, and gypsum powder 3-D print
40 x 40 x 80 in. (100 x 100 x 200 cm)
Courtesy the artist

Anicka Yi

After Democracy, 2016
Silicone on panel, artificial flowers, and
nylon filament
36 x 24 x 4 in. (91.4 x 61 x 10.2 cm)
Collection Nasiba and Thomas Hartland-Mackie

Childless Comfort, 2016
Silicone on panel, artificial flowers, and
nylon filament
41¾ x 28 x 3½ in. (106 x 71.1 x 9 cm)
Collection Marguerite Steed Hoffman

Our Brand Is Crisis, 2016
Silicone on panel, artificial flowers, and
nylon filament
36 x 24 x 4 in. (91.4 x 61 x 10.2 cm)
Collection Fern and Lenard Tessler

Eugenie Brinkema is associate professor of contemporary literature and media at MIT. Her research in film and media studies focuses on violence, affect, sexuality, and aesthetics; she is the author of *The Forms of the Affects* (2014, Duke University Press). Brinkema's articles have appeared in numerous anthologies and journals, including *Angelaki*, *Camera Obscura*, *Criticism*, *differences*, *Discourse*, the *Journal of Speculative Philosophy*, the *Journal of Visual Culture*, *Qui Parle*, *Screen*, and *World Picture*. Her current project, *Algebras of Sensation*, explores the theoretical potential of radical formalism in relation to horror and love.

Henriette Huldisch is the curator at the MIT List Visual Arts Center. Previously, she was curator at Hamburger Bahnhof, Museum for Contemporary Art, Berlin, and assistant curator at the Whitney Museum of American Art, New York. Her publications include *Tala Madani: First Light* (2016, DelMonico Books • Prestel) and *Rosa Barba: The Color Out of Space* (2016, Dancing Foxes Press). Her writing also has appeared in periodicals and anthologies such as *Artforum* and *What Ever Happened to New Institutionalism?* (2016, Sternberg Press).

Johanna Burton is Keith Haring Director and Curator of Education and Public Engagement at the New Museum, New York. Prior to holding this position, she was the director of the graduate program at the Center for Curatorial Studies, Bard College, and associate director and senior faculty member at the Whitney Museum of American Art's Independent Study Program. Her writing has appeared in publications including *Artforum*, *October*, and *Texte zur Kunst*.

Emily Watlington is the curatorial research assistant at the MIT List Visual Arts Center, and a master of science in architecture studies (SMArchS) candidate in the History, Theory, and Criticism of Art + Architecture Department at MIT. Her art criticism has appeared in periodicals such as *Mousse Magazine* and *Art Papers*, and her article on Ryan Trecartin's high school art is forthcoming in the edited volume *Analogue Living in a Digital World* (2017, Tasmeem Doha).

Andrea Büttner
Sophie Calle
Casey Kaplan Gallery, New York
Alejandro Cesarco
David Kordansky Gallery, Los Angeles
Jason Dodge
ESSEX STREET, New York
Galleri Riis, Oslo
Alex Hank, Los Angeles
Nasiba and Thomas Hartland-Mackie, Dallas
Antonia Hirsch
Marguerite Steed Hoffman, Dallas
Hollybush Gardens, London
Labor, Mexico City
Jill Magid
Park McArthur
Overduin & Co., Los Angeles
Paula Cooper Gallery, New York
Private collection, New York, loan coordinated by the
        Felix Gonzalez-Torres Foundation, New York
Republic Gallery, Vancouver
Carlomar Rios, New York
Lisa Tan
Tanya Leighton Gallery, Berlin
Fern and Lenard Tessler, New York
Untilthen, Paris
Erika Vogt
Susanne M. Winterling

Advisory Committee

Geoffrey L. Hargadon,
Chair
Karen Arenson
Lindsay Coolidge
Brit d'Arbeloff
John Durant
Carolyn Fine Friedman
John Frishkopf
Susanne Ghez
John Guttag
Drew Katz
Philip Khoury
Leila Kinney
Marian Marill
Lucy Moon-Lim
Stephen Prina
Murray Robinson
Sebastian Schmidt
Jeanne D. Stanton
Martin E. Zimmerman

Staff

Susie Allen
Karen S. Fegley
Magda Fernandez
Emily A. Garner
Paul C. Ha
Henriette Huldisch
Kristin Johnson
Mark Linga
Tim Lloyd
Tricia Murray
John Osorio-Buck
Amy Patacchiola
Kevin Smith
Yuri Stone
Ariana Webber
Suara Welitoff
Betsy Willett

Pages 41–43: © 2017 Andrea Büttner / VG Bild-Kunst, Bonn. Pages 45 and 47: © 2017 Sophie Calle / Artists Rights Society (ARS), New York / ADAGP, Paris; images courtesy Sophie Calle and Paula Cooper Gallery, New York; photo: Steven Probert. Pages 48–51: Courtesy the artist and Tanya Leighton Gallery, Berlin; © Alejandro Cesarco. Page 55: © The Felix Gonzalez-Torres Foundation; image courtesy Andrea Rosen Gallery, New York; installation view: *Felix Gonzalez-Torres: This Place*; Metropolitan Arts Centre, Belfast, Northern Ireland; October 30, 2015–January 24, 2016; curated by Eoin Dara. Pages 57–59: © Antonia Hirsch. Pages 61–63: Courtesy the artist and Labor, Mexico City; installation view: *Woman With Sombrero*, Art in General, New York, 2013; photo: © 2013 Steven Probert. Pages 65–67: Installation views: *Poly*, Chisenhale Gallery, London, 2016; photos: Mark Blower. Pages 69–71: Installation views: *Lisa Tan: For Every Word Has Its Own Shadow*, Galleri Riis, Stockholm, 2015; images courtesy the artist and Galleri Riis, Oslo and Stockholm. Pages 73–75: © Erika Vogt. Pages 77 and 79: Installation views: *ESPONJA* at SOLO SHOWS, São Paulo, 2015. Pages 81–83: © Anicka Yi; images courtesy the artist; 47 Canal, New York; and Fridericianum, Kassel; photos: Fabian Frinzel and Joerg Lohse.

This catalogue is published on the occasion of the exhibition *An Inventory of Shimmers: Objects of Intimacy in Contemporary Art,* organized for the MIT List Visual Arts Center by Henriette Huldisch and on view from May 19 to July 16, 2017.

Exhibitions at the List Center are made possible with the support of Jane and Neil Pappalardo, Cynthia and John Reed, and Terry and Rick Stone. *An Inventory of Shimmers: Objects of Intimacy in Contemporary Art* is generously supported by the Andy Warhol Foundation for the Visual Arts.

General operating support is provided by the Massachusetts Institute of Technology (MIT), the Council for the Arts at MIT, the Office of the Associate Provost at MIT, the MIT School of Architecture + Planning, the Massachusetts Cultural Council, and many generous individual donors. The Advisory Committee Members of the List Visual Arts Center are gratefully acknowledged.

Editor: Anne Ray
Design: Miko McGinty, Rita Jules, and
	Claire Bidwell
Typesetting: Tina Henderson
Printed in the United States by Puritan Capital,
	Hollis, New Hampshire

Published in 2017 by the MIT List Visual Arts Center and DelMonico Books • Prestel

Library of Congress control number: 2017935988

A CIP catalogue record for this book is available from the British Library.

ISBN: 978-3-7913-5611-2

DelMonico Books, an imprint of Prestel Publishing, a member of Verlagsgruppe Random House GmbH

Prestel Verlag
Neumarkter Strasse 28
81573 Munich

Prestel Publishing Ltd.
14–17 Wells Street
London W1T 3PD

Prestel Publishing
900 Broadway, Suite 603
New York, NY 10003

www.prestel.com

MIT List Visual Arts Center
Wiesner Building
20 Ames Street
Cambridge, MA 02139
+1 617 253 4680

www.listart.mit.edu